Y0-BYZ-213

ISBN 0-8373-2361-4

C-2361   CAREER EXAMINATION SERIES

This is your
PASSBOOK® for...

Animal Shelter Officer

Test Preparation Study Guide

Questions & Answers

NLC

NATIONAL LEARNING CORPORATION

PASSBOOK®

NOTICE

PASSBOOK SERIES®

THE *PASSBOOK SERIES®* has been created to prepare applicants and candidates for the ultimate academic battlefield – the examination room.

At some time in our lives, each and every one of us may be required to take an examination – for validation, matriculation, admission, qualification, registration, certification, or licensure.

Based on the assumption that every applicant or candidate has met the basic formal educational standards, has taken the required number of courses, and read the necessary texts, the *PASSBOOK SERIES®* furnishes the one special preparation which may assure passing with confidence, instead of failing with insecurity. Examination questions – together with answers – are furnished as the basic vehicle for study so that the mysteries of the examination and its compounding difficulties may be eliminated or diminished by a sure method.

This book is meant to help you pass your examination provided that you qualify and are serious in your objective.

The entire field is reviewed through the huge store of content information which is succinctly presented through a provocative and challenging approach – the question-and-answer method.

A climate of success is established by furnishing the correct answers at the end of each test.

You soon learn to recognize types of questions, forms of questions, and patterns of questioning. You may even begin to anticipate expected outcomes.

You perceive that many questions are repeated or adapted so that you can gain acute insights, which may enable you to score many sure points.

You learn how to confront new questions, or types of questions, and to attack them confidently and work out the correct answers.

You note objectives and emphases, and recognize pitfalls and dangers, so that you may make positive educational adjustments.

Moreover, you are kept fully informed in relation to new concepts, methods, practices, and directions in the field.

You discover that you are actually taking the examination all the time: you are preparing for the examination by "taking" an examination, not by reading extraneous and/or supererogatory textbooks.

In short, this PASSBOOK®, used directedly, should be an important factor in helping you to pass your test.

ANIMAL SHELTER OFFICER

DUTIES
Performs routine work in the care and handling of animals and in the maintenance of an animal shelter; performs related work as required.

SCOPE OF THE WRITTEN TEST
The written test will be designed to test for knowledge, skills, and/or abilities in such areas as:
1. Care and handling of dogs and small animals;
2. Clerical aptitude; and
3. Understanding and interpreting written material.

———

HOW TO TAKE A TEST

I. YOU MUST PASS AN EXAMINATION

A. *WHAT EVERY CANDIDATE SHOULD KNOW*

Examination applicants often ask us for help in preparing for the written test. What can I study in advance? What kinds of questions will be asked? How will the test be given? How will the papers be graded?

As an applicant for a civil service examination, you may be wondering about some of these things. Our purpose here is to suggest effective methods of advance study and to describe civil service examinations.

Your chances for success on this examination can be increased if you know how to prepare. Those "pre-examination jitters" can be reduced if you know what to expect. You can even experience an adventure in good citizenship if you know why civil service exams are given.

B. *WHY ARE CIVIL SERVICE EXAMINATIONS GIVEN?*

Civil service examinations are important to you in two ways. As a citizen, you want public jobs filled by employees who know how to do their work. As a job seeker, you want a fair chance to compete for that job on an equal footing with other candidates. The best-known means of accomplishing this two-fold goal is the competitive examination.

Exams are widely publicized throughout the nation. They may be administered for jobs in federal, state, city, municipal, town or village governments or agencies.

Any citizen may apply, with some limitations, such as the age or residence of applicants. Your experience and education may be reviewed to see whether you meet the requirements for the particular examination. When these requirements exist, they are reasonable and applied consistently to all applicants. Thus, a competitive examination may cause you some uneasiness now, but it is your privilege and safeguard.

C. *HOW ARE CIVIL SERVICE EXAMS DEVELOPED?*

Examinations are carefully written by trained technicians who are specialists in the field known as "psychological measurement," in consultation with recognized authorities in the field of work that the test will cover. These experts recommend the subject matter areas or skills to be tested; only those knowledges or skills important to your success on the job are included. The most reliable books and source materials available are used as references. Together, the experts and technicians judge the difficulty level of the questions.

Test technicians know how to phrase questions so that the problem is clearly stated. Their ethics do not permit "trick" or "catch" questions. Questions may have been tried out on sample groups, or subjected to statistical analysis, to determine their usefulness.

Written tests are often used in combination with performance tests, ratings of training and experience, and oral interviews. All of these measures combine to form the best-known means of finding the right person for the right job.

II. HOW TO PASS THE WRITTEN TEST

A. NATURE OF THE EXAMINATION

To prepare intelligently for civil service examinations, you should know how they differ from school examinations you have taken. In school you were assigned certain definite pages to read or subjects to cover. The examination questions were quite detailed and usually emphasized memory. Civil service exams, on the other hand, try to discover your present ability to perform the duties of a position, plus your potentiality to learn these duties. In other words, a civil service exam attempts to predict how successful you will be. Questions cover such a broad area that they cannot be as minute and detailed as school exam questions.

In the public service similar kinds of work, or positions, are grouped together in one "class." This process is known as *position-classification*. All the positions in a class are paid according to the salary range for that class. One class title covers all of these positions, and they are all tested by the same examination.

B. FOUR BASIC STEPS

1) Study the announcement

How, then, can you know what subjects to study? Our best answer is: "Learn as much as possible about the class of positions for which you've applied." The exam will test the knowledge, skills and abilities needed to do the work.

Your most valuable source of information about the position you want is the official exam announcement. This announcement lists the training and experience qualifications. Check these standards and apply only if you come reasonably close to meeting them.

The brief description of the position in the examination announcement offers some clues to the subjects which will be tested. Think about the job itself. Review the duties in your mind. Can you perform them, or are there some in which you are rusty? Fill in the blank spots in your preparation.

Many jurisdictions preview the written test in the exam announcement by including a section called "Knowledge and Abilities Required," "Scope of the Examination," or some similar heading. Here you will find out specifically what fields will be tested.

2) Review your own background

Once you learn in general what the position is all about, and what you need to know to do the work, ask yourself which subjects you already know fairly well and which need improvement. You may wonder whether to concentrate on improving your strong areas or on building some background in your fields of weakness. When the announcement has specified "some knowledge" or "considerable knowledge," or has used adjectives like "beginning principles of..." or "advanced ... methods," you can get a clue as to the number and difficulty of questions to be asked in any given field. More questions, and hence broader coverage, would be included for those subjects which are more important in the work. Now weigh your strengths and weaknesses against the job requirements and prepare accordingly.

3) Determine the level of the position

Another way to tell how intensively you should prepare is to understand the level of the job for which you are applying. Is it the entering level? In other words, is this the position in which beginners in a field of work are hired? Or is it an intermediate or advanced level? Sometimes this is indicated by such words as "Junior" or "Senior" in the class title. Other jurisdictions use Roman numerals to designate the level – Clerk I, Clerk II, for example. The word "Supervisor" sometimes appears in the title. If the level is not indicated by the title, check the description of duties. Will you be working under very close supervision, or will you have responsibility for independent decisions in this work?

4) Choose appropriate study materials

Now that you know the subjects to be examined and the relative amount of each subject to be covered, you can choose suitable study materials. For beginning level jobs, or even advanced ones, if you have a pronounced weakness in some aspect of your training, read a modern, standard textbook in that field. Be sure it is up to date and has general coverage. Such books are normally available at your library, and the librarian will be glad to help you locate one. For entry-level positions, questions of appropriate difficulty are chosen – neither highly advanced questions, nor those too simple. Such questions require careful thought but not advanced training.

If the position for which you are applying is technical or advanced, you will read more advanced, specialized material. If you are already familiar with the basic principles of your field, elementary textbooks would waste your time. Concentrate on advanced textbooks and technical periodicals. Think through the concepts and review difficult problems in your field.

These are all general sources. You can get more ideas on your own initiative, following these leads. For example, training manuals and publications of the government agency which employs workers in your field can be useful, particularly for technical and professional positions. A letter or visit to the government department involved may result in more specific study suggestions, and certainly will provide you with a more definite idea of the exact nature of the position you are seeking.

III. KINDS OF TESTS

Tests are used for purposes other than measuring knowledge and ability to perform specified duties. For some positions, it is equally important to test ability to make adjustments to new situations or to profit from training. In others, basic mental abilities not dependent on information are essential. Questions which test these things may not appear as pertinent to the duties of the position as those which test for knowledge and information. Yet they are often highly important parts of a fair examination. For very general questions, it is almost impossible to help you direct your study efforts. What we can do is to point out some of the more common of these general abilities needed in public service positions and describe some typical questions.

1) General information

Broad, general information has been found useful for predicting job success in some kinds of work. This is tested in a variety of ways, from vocabulary lists to questions about current events. Basic background in some field of work, such as sociology or economics, may be sampled in a group of questions. Often these are principles which have become familiar to most persons through exposure rather than through formal training. It is difficult to advise you how to study for these questions; being alert to the world around you is our best suggestion.

2) Verbal ability

An example of an ability needed in many positions is verbal or language ability. Verbal ability is, in brief, the ability to use and understand words. Vocabulary and grammar tests are typical measures of this ability. Reading comprehension or paragraph interpretation questions are common in many kinds of civil service tests. You are given a paragraph of written material and asked to find its central meaning.

3) Numerical ability

Number skills can be tested by the familiar arithmetic problem, by checking paired lists of numbers to see which are alike and which are different, or by interpreting charts and graphs. In the latter test, a graph may be printed in the test booklet which you are asked to use as the basis for answering questions.

4) Observation

A popular test for law-enforcement positions is the observation test. A picture is shown to you for several minutes, then taken away. Questions about the picture test your ability to observe both details and larger elements.

5) Following directions

In many positions in the public service, the employee must be able to carry out written instructions dependably and accurately. You may be given a chart with several columns, each column listing a variety of information. The questions require you to carry out directions involving the information given in the chart.

6) Skills and aptitudes

Performance tests effectively measure some manual skills and aptitudes. When the skill is one in which you are trained, such as typing or shorthand, you can practice. These tests are often very much like those given in business school or high school courses. For many of the other skills and aptitudes, however, no short-time preparation can be made. Skills and abilities natural to you or that you have developed throughout your lifetime are being tested.

Many of the general questions just described provide all the data needed to answer the questions and ask you to use your reasoning ability to find the answers. Your best preparation for these tests, as well as for tests of facts and ideas, is to be at your physical and mental best. You, no doubt, have your own methods of getting into an exam-taking mood and keeping "in shape." The next section lists some ideas on this subject.

IV. KINDS OF QUESTIONS

Only rarely is the "essay" question, which you answer in narrative form, used in civil service tests. Civil service tests are usually of the short-answer type. Full instructions for answering these questions will be given to you at the examination. But in case this is your first experience with short-answer questions and separate answer sheets, here is what you need to know:

1) Multiple-choice Questions

Most popular of the short-answer questions is the "multiple choice" or "best answer" question. It can be used, for example, to test for factual knowledge, ability to solve problems or judgment in meeting situations found at work.

A multiple-choice question is normally one of three types—

- It can begin with an incomplete statement followed by several possible endings. You are to find the one ending which *best* completes the statement, although some of the others may not be entirely wrong.
- It can also be a complete statement in the form of a question which is answered by choosing one of the statements listed.
- It can be in the form of a problem – again you select the best answer.

Here is an example of a multiple-choice question with a discussion which should give you some clues as to the method for choosing the right answer:

> When an employee has a complaint about his assignment, the action which will *best* help him overcome his difficulty is to
> A. discuss his difficulty with his coworkers
> B. take the problem to the head of the organization
> C. take the problem to the person who gave him the assignment
> D. say nothing to anyone about his complaint

In answering this question, you should study each of the choices to find which is best. Consider choice "A" – Certainly an employee may discuss his complaint with fellow employees, but no change or improvement can result, and the complaint remains unresolved. Choice "B" is a poor choice since the head of the organization probably does not know what assignment you have been given, and taking your problem to him is known as "going over the head" of the supervisor. The supervisor, or person who made the assignment, is the person who can clarify it or correct any injustice. Choice "C" is, therefore, correct. To say nothing, as in choice "D," is unwise. Supervisors have and interest in knowing the problems employees are facing, and the employee is seeking a solution to his problem.

2) True/False Questions

The "true/false" or "right/wrong" form of question is sometimes used. Here a complete statement is given. Your job is to decide whether the statement is right or wrong.

SAMPLE: A person-to-person long-distance telephone call costs less than a station-to-station call to the same city.

This statement is wrong, or false, since person-to-person calls are more expensive.

This is not a complete list of all possible question forms, although most of the others are variations of these common types. You will always get complete directions for answering questions. Be sure you understand *how* to mark your answers – ask questions until you do.

V. RECORDING YOUR ANSWERS

For an examination with very few applicants, you may be told to record your answers in the test booklet itself. Separate answer sheets are much more common. If this separate answer sheet is to be scored by machine – and this is often the case – it is highly important that you mark your answers correctly in order to get credit.

An electric scoring machine is often used in civil service offices because of the speed with which papers can be scored. Machine-scored answer sheets must be marked with a pencil, which will be given to you. This pencil has a high graphite content which responds to the electric scoring machine. As a matter of fact, stray dots may register as answers, so do not let your pencil rest on the answer sheet while you are pondering the correct answer. Also, if your pencil lead breaks or is otherwise defective, ask for another.

Since the answer sheet will be dropped in a slot in the scoring machine, be careful not to bend the corners or get the paper crumpled.

The answer sheet normally has five vertical columns of numbers, with 30 numbers to a column. These numbers correspond to the question numbers in your test booklet. After each number, going across the page are four or five pairs of dotted lines. These short dotted lines have small letters or numbers above them. The first two pairs may also have a "T" or "F" above the letters. This indicates that the first two pairs only are to be used if the questions are of the true-false type. If the questions are multiple choice, disregard the "T" and "F" and pay attention only to the small letters or numbers.

Answer your questions in the manner of the sample that follows:

32. The largest city in the United States is
    A. Washington, D.C.
    B. New York City
    C. Chicago
    D. Detroit
    E. San Francisco

1) Choose the answer you think is best. (New York City is the largest, so "B" is correct.)
2) Find the row of dotted lines numbered the same as the question you are answering. (Find row number 32)
3) Find the pair of dotted lines corresponding to the answer. (Find the pair of lines under the mark "B.")
4) Make a solid black mark between the dotted lines.

VI. BEFORE THE TEST

Common sense will help you find procedures to follow to get ready for an examination. Too many of us, however, overlook these sensible measures. Indeed, nervousness and fatigue have been found to be the most serious reasons why applicants fail to do their best on civil service tests. Here is a list of reminders:

- Begin your preparation early – Don't wait until the last minute to go scurrying around for books and materials or to find out what the position is all about.
- Prepare continuously – An hour a night for a week is better than an all-night cram session. This has been definitely established. What is more, a night a

week for a month will return better dividends than crowding your study into a shorter period of time.

- Locate the place of the exam – You have been sent a notice telling you when and where to report for the examination. If the location is in a different town or otherwise unfamiliar to you, it would be well to inquire the best route and learn something about the building.
- Relax the night before the test – Allow your mind to rest. Do not study at all that night. Plan some mild recreation or diversion; then go to bed early and get a good night's sleep.
- Get up early enough to make a leisurely trip to the place for the test – This way unforeseen events, traffic snarls, unfamiliar buildings, etc. will not upset you.
- Dress comfortably – A written test is not a fashion show. You will be known by number and not by name, so wear something comfortable.
- Leave excess paraphernalia at home – Shopping bags and odd bundles will get in your way. You need bring only the items mentioned in the official notice you received; usually everything you need is provided. Do not bring reference books to the exam. They will only confuse those last minutes and be taken away from you when in the test room.
- Arrive somewhat ahead of time – If because of transportation schedules you must get there very early, bring a newspaper or magazine to take your mind off yourself while waiting.
- Locate the examination room – When you have found the proper room, you will be directed to the seat or part of the room where you will sit. Sometimes you are given a sheet of instructions to read while you are waiting. Do not fill out any forms until you are told to do so; just read them and be prepared.
- Relax and prepare to listen to the instructions
- If you have any physical problem that may keep you from doing your best, be sure to tell the test administrator. If you are sick or in poor health, you really cannot do your best on the exam. You can come back and take the test some other time.

VII. AT THE TEST

The day of the test is here and you have the test booklet in your hand. The temptation to get going is very strong. Caution! There is more to success than knowing the right answers. You must know how to identify your papers and understand variations in the type of short-answer question used in this particular examination. Follow these suggestions for maximum results from your efforts:

1) Cooperate with the monitor

The test administrator has a duty to create a situation in which you can be as much at ease as possible. He will give instructions, tell you when to begin, check to see that you are marking your answer sheet correctly, and so on. He is not there to guard you, although he will see that your competitors do not take unfair advantage. He wants to help you do your best.

2) Listen to all instructions

Don't jump the gun! Wait until you understand all directions. In most civil service tests you get more time than you need to answer the questions. So don't be in a hurry.

Read each word of instructions until you clearly understand the meaning. Study the examples, listen to all announcements and follow directions. Ask questions if you do not understand what to do.

3) Identify your papers

Civil service exams are usually identified by number only. You will be assigned a number; you must not put your name on your test papers. Be sure to copy your number correctly. Since more than one exam may be given, copy your exact examination title.

4) Plan your time

Unless you are told that a test is a "speed" or "rate of work" test, speed itself is usually not important. Time enough to answer all the questions will be provided, but this does not mean that you have all day. An overall time limit has been set. Divide the total time (in minutes) by the number of questions to determine the approximate time you have for each question.

5) Do not linger over difficult questions

If you come across a difficult question, mark it with a paper clip (useful to have along) and come back to it when you have been through the booklet. One caution if you do this – be sure to skip a number on your answer sheet as well. Check often to be sure that you have not lost your place and that you are marking in the row numbered the same as the question you are answering.

6) Read the questions

Be sure you know what the question asks! Many capable people are unsuccessful because they failed to *read* the questions correctly.

7) Answer all questions

Unless you have been instructed that a penalty will be deducted for incorrect answers, it is better to guess than to omit a question.

8) Speed tests

It is often better NOT to guess on speed tests. It has been found that on timed tests people are tempted to spend the last few seconds before time is called in marking answers at random – without even reading them – in the hope of picking up a few extra points. To discourage this practice, the instructions may warn you that your score will be "corrected" for guessing. That is, a penalty will be applied. The incorrect answers will be deducted from the correct ones, or some other penalty formula will be used.

9) Review your answers

If you finish before time is called, go back to the questions you guessed or omitted to give them further thought. Review other answers if you have time.

10) Return your test materials

If you are ready to leave before others have finished or time is called, take ALL your materials to the monitor and leave quietly. Never take any test material with you. The monitor can discover whose papers are not complete, and taking a test booklet may be grounds for disqualification.

VIII. EXAMINATION TECHNIQUES

1) Read the general instructions carefully. These are usually printed on the first page of the exam booklet. As a rule, these instructions refer to the timing of the examination; the fact that you should not start work until the signal and must stop work at a signal, etc. If there are any *special* instructions, such as a choice of questions to be answered, make sure that you note this instruction carefully.

2) When you are ready to start work on the examination, that is as soon as the signal has been given, read the instructions to each question booklet, underline any key words or phrases, such as *least, best, outline, describe* and the like. In this way you will tend to answer as requested rather than discover on reviewing your paper that you *listed without describing*, that you selected the *worst* choice rather than the *best* choice, etc.

3) If the examination is of the objective or multiple-choice type – that is, each question will also give a series of possible answers: A, B, C or D, and you are called upon to select the best answer and write the letter next to that answer on your answer paper – it is advisable to start answering each question in turn. There may be anywhere from 50 to 100 such questions in the three or four hours allotted and you can see how much time would be taken if you read through all the questions before beginning to answer any. Furthermore, if you come across a question or group of questions which you know would be difficult to answer, it would undoubtedly affect your handling of all the other questions.

4) If the examination is of the essay type and contains but a few questions, it is a moot point as to whether you should read all the questions before starting to answer any one. Of course, if you are given a choice – say five out of seven and the like – then it is essential to read all the questions so you can eliminate the two that are most difficult. If, however, you are asked to answer all the questions, there may be danger in trying to answer the easiest one first because you may find that you will spend too much time on it. The best technique is to answer the first question, then proceed to the second, etc.

5) Time your answers. Before the exam begins, write down the time it started, then add the time allowed for the examination and write down the time it must be completed, then divide the time available somewhat as follows:
   - If 3-1/2 hours are allowed, that would be 210 minutes. If you have 80 objective-type questions, that would be an average of 2-1/2 minutes per question. Allow yourself no more than 2 minutes per question, or a total of 160 minutes, which will permit about 50 minutes to review.
   - If for the time allotment of 210 minutes there are 7 essay questions to answer, that would average about 30 minutes a question. Give yourself only 25 minutes per question so that you have about 35 minutes to review.

6) The most important instruction is to *read each question* and make sure you know what is wanted. The second most important instruction is to *time yourself properly* so that you answer every question. The third most

important instruction is to *answer every question*. Guess if you have to but include something for each question. Remember that you will receive no credit for a blank and will probably receive some credit if you write something in answer to an essay question. If you guess a letter – say "B" for a multiple-choice question – you may have guessed right. If you leave a blank as an answer to a multiple-choice question, the examiners may respect your feelings but it will not add a point to your score. Some exams may penalize you for wrong answers, so in such cases *only*, you may not want to guess unless you have some basis for your answer.

7) Suggestions
   a. Objective-type questions
      1. Examine the question booklet for proper sequence of pages and questions
      2. Read all instructions carefully
      3. Skip any question which seems too difficult; return to it after all other questions have been answered
      4. Apportion your time properly; do not spend too much time on any single question or group of questions
      5. Note and underline key words – *all, most, fewest, least, best, worst, same, opposite,* etc.
      6. Pay particular attention to negatives
      7. Note unusual option, e.g., unduly long, short, complex, different or similar in content to the body of the question
      8. Observe the use of "hedging" words – *probably, may, most likely,* etc.
      9. Make sure that your answer is put next to the same number as the question
      10. Do not second-guess unless you have good reason to believe the second answer is definitely more correct
      11. Cross out original answer if you decide another answer is more accurate; do not erase until you are ready to hand your paper in
      12. Answer all questions; guess unless instructed otherwise
      13. Leave time for review

   b. Essay questions
      1. Read each question carefully
      2. Determine exactly what is wanted. Underline key words or phrases.
      3. Decide on outline or paragraph answer
      4. Include many different points and elements unless asked to develop any one or two points or elements
      5. Show impartiality by giving pros and cons unless directed to select one side only
      6. Make and write down any assumptions you find necessary to answer the questions
      7. Watch your English, grammar, punctuation and choice of words
      8. Time your answers; don't crowd material

8) Answering the essay question

Most essay questions can be answered by framing the specific response around several key words or ideas. Here are a few such key words or ideas:

M's: manpower, materials, methods, money, management
P's: purpose, program, policy, plan, procedure, practice, problems, pitfalls, personnel, public relations

    a. Six basic steps in handling problems:
1. Preliminary plan and background development
2. Collect information, data and facts
3. Analyze and interpret information, data and facts
4. Analyze and develop solutions as well as make recommendations
5. Prepare report and sell recommendations
6. Install recommendations and follow up effectiveness

    b. Pitfalls to avoid
1. *Taking things for granted* – A statement of the situation does not necessarily imply that each of the elements is necessarily true; for example, a complaint may be invalid and biased so that all that can be taken for granted is that a complaint has been registered
2. *Considering only one side of a situation* – Wherever possible, indicate several alternatives and then point out the reasons you selected the best one
3. *Failing to indicate follow up* – Whenever your answer indicates action on your part, make certain that you will take proper follow-up action to see how successful your recommendations, procedures or actions turn out to be
4. *Taking too long in answering any single question* – Remember to time your answers properly

IX. AFTER THE TEST

Scoring procedures differ in detail among civil service jurisdictions although the general principles are the same. Whether the papers are hand-scored or graded by machine we have described, they are nearly always graded by number. That is, the person who marks the paper knows only the number – never the name – of the applicant. Not until all the papers have been graded will they be matched with names. If other tests, such as training and experience or oral interview ratings have been given, scores will be combined. Different parts of the examination usually have different weights. For example, the written test might count 60 percent of the final grade, and a rating of training and experience 40 percent. In many jurisdictions, veterans will have a certain number of points added to their grades.

After the final grade has been determined, the names are placed in grade order and an eligible list is established. There are various methods for resolving ties between those who get the same final grade – probably the most common is to place first the name of the person whose application was received first. Job offers are made from the eligible list in the order the names appear on it. You will be notified of your grade and your rank as soon as all these computations have been made. This will be done as rapidly as possible.

People who are found to meet the requirements in the announcement are called "eligibles." Their names are put on a list of eligible candidates. An eligible's chances of getting a job depend on how high he stands on this list and how fast agencies are filling jobs from the list.

When a job is to be filled from a list of eligibles, the agency asks for the names of people on the list of eligibles for that job. When the civil service commission receives this request, it sends to the agency the names of the three people highest on this list. Or, if the job to be filled has specialized requirements, the office sends the agency the names of the top three persons who meet these requirements from the general list.

The appointing officer makes a choice from among the three people whose names were sent to him. If the selected person accepts the appointment, the names of the others are put back on the list to be considered for future openings.

That is the rule in hiring from all kinds of eligible lists, whether they are for typist, carpenter, chemist, or something else. For every vacancy, the appointing officer has his choice of any one of the top three eligibles on the list. This explains why the person whose name is on top of the list sometimes does not get an appointment when some of the persons lower on the list do. If the appointing officer chooses the second or third eligible, the No. 1 eligible does not get a job at once, but stays on the list until he is appointed or the list is terminated.

X. HOW TO PASS THE INTERVIEW TEST

The examination for which you applied requires an oral interview test. You have already taken the written test and you are now being called for the interview test – the final part of the formal examination.

You may think that it is not possible to prepare for an interview test and that there are no procedures to follow during an interview. Our purpose is to point out some things you can do in advance that will help you and some good rules to follow and pitfalls to avoid while you are being interviewed.

What is an interview supposed to test?

The written examination is designed to test the technical knowledge and competence of the candidate; the oral is designed to evaluate intangible qualities, not readily measured otherwise, and to establish a list showing the relative fitness of each candidate – as measured against his competitors – for the position sought. Scoring is not on the basis of "right" and "wrong," but on a sliding scale of values ranging from "not passable" to "outstanding." As a matter of fact, it is possible to achieve a relatively low score without a single "incorrect" answer because of evident weakness in the qualities being measured.

Occasionally, an examination may consist entirely of an oral test – either an individual or a group oral. In such cases, information is sought concerning the technical knowledges and abilities of the candidate, since there has been no written examination for this purpose. More commonly, however, an oral test is used to supplement a written examination.

Who conducts interviews?

The composition of oral boards varies among different jurisdictions. In nearly all, a representative of the personnel department serves as chairman. One of the members of the board may be a representative of the department in which the candidate would work. In some cases, "outside experts" are used, and, frequently, a businessman or some other representative of the general public is asked to serve. Labor and management or other special groups may be represented. The aim is to secure the services of experts in the appropriate field.

However the board is composed, it is a good idea (and not at all improper or unethical) to ascertain in advance of the interview who the members are and what groups they represent. When you are introduced to them, you will have some idea of their backgrounds and interests, and at least you will not stutter and stammer over their names.

What should be done before the interview?

While knowledge about the board members is useful and takes some of the surprise element out of the interview, there is other preparation which is more substantive. It *is* possible to prepare for an oral interview – in several ways:

1) Keep a copy of your application and review it carefully before the interview

This may be the only document before the oral board, and the starting point of the interview. Know what education and experience you have listed there, and the sequence and dates of all of it. Sometimes the board will ask you to review the highlights of your experience for them; you should not have to hem and haw doing it.

2) Study the class specification and the examination announcement

Usually, the oral board has one or both of these to guide them. The qualities, characteristics or knowledges required by the position sought are stated in these documents. They offer valuable clues as to the nature of the oral interview. For example, if the job involves supervisory responsibilities, the announcement will usually indicate that knowledge of modern supervisory methods and the qualifications of the candidate as a supervisor will be tested. If so, you can expect such questions, frequently in the form of a hypothetical situation which you are expected to solve. NEVER go into an oral without knowledge of the duties and responsibilities of the job you seek.

3) Think through each qualification required

Try to visualize the kind of questions you would ask if you were a board member. How well could you answer them? Try especially to appraise your own knowledge and background in each area, *measured against the job sought*, and identify any areas in which you are weak. Be critical and realistic – do not flatter yourself.

4) Do some general reading in areas in which you feel you may be weak

For example, if the job involves supervision and your past experience has NOT, some general reading in supervisory methods and practices, particularly in the field of human relations, might be useful. Do NOT study agency procedures or detailed manuals. The oral board will be testing your understanding and capacity, not your memory.

5) Get a good night's sleep and watch your general health and mental attitude

You will want a clear head at the interview. Take care of a cold or any other minor ailment, and of course, no hangovers.

What should be done on the day of the interview?

Now comes the day of the interview itself. Give yourself plenty of time to get there. Plan to arrive somewhat ahead of the scheduled time, particularly if your appointment is in the fore part of the day. If a previous candidate fails to appear, the board might be ready for you a bit early. By early afternoon an oral board is almost invariably behind schedule if there are many candidates, and you may have to wait.

Take along a book or magazine to read, or your application to review, but leave any extraneous material in the waiting room when you go in for your interview. In any event, relax and compose yourself.

The matter of dress is important. The board is forming impressions about you – from your experience, your manners, your attitude, and your appearance. Give your personal appearance careful attention. Dress your best, but not your flashiest. Choose conservative, appropriate clothing, and be sure it is immaculate. This is a business interview, and your appearance should indicate that you regard it as such. Besides, being well groomed and properly dressed will help boost your confidence.

Sooner or later, someone will call your name and escort you into the interview room. *This is it.* From here on you are on your own. It is too late for any more preparation. But remember, you asked for this opportunity to prove your fitness, and you are here because your request was granted.

What happens when you go in?

The usual sequence of events will be as follows: The clerk (who is often the board stenographer) will introduce you to the chairman of the oral board, who will introduce you to the other members of the board. Acknowledge the introductions before you sit down. Do not be surprised if you find a microphone facing you or a stenotypist sitting by. Oral interviews are usually recorded in the event of an appeal or other review.

Usually the chairman of the board will open the interview by reviewing the highlights of your education and work experience from your application – primarily for the benefit of the other members of the board, as well as to get the material into the record. Do not interrupt or comment unless there is an error or significant misinterpretation; if that is the case, do not hesitate. But do not quibble about insignificant matters. Also, he will usually ask you some question about your education, experience or your present job – partly to get you to start talking and to establish the interviewing "rapport." He may start the actual questioning, or turn it over to one of the other members. Frequently, each member undertakes the questioning on a particular area, one in which he is perhaps most competent, so you can expect each member to participate in the examination. Because time is limited, you may also expect some rather abrupt switches in the direction the questioning takes, so do not be upset by it. Normally, a board member will not pursue a single line of questioning unless he discovers a particular strength or weakness.

After each member has participated, the chairman will usually ask whether any member has any further questions, then will ask you if you have anything you wish to add. Unless you are expecting this question, it may floor you. Worse, it may start you off on an extended, extemporaneous speech. The board is not usually seeking more information. The question is principally to offer you a last opportunity to present further qualifications or to indicate that you have nothing to add. So, if you feel that a significant qualification or characteristic has been overlooked, it is proper to point it out in a sentence or so. Do not compliment the board on the thoroughness of their examination – they have been sketchy, and you know it. If you wish, merely say, "No thank you, I have nothing further to add." This is a point where you can "talk yourself out" of a good impression or fail to present an important bit of information. Remember, *you close the interview yourself.*

The chairman will then say, "That is all, Mr. _____, thank you." Do not be startled; the interview is over, and quicker than you think. Thank him, gather your belongings and take your leave. Save your sigh of relief for the other side of the door.

How to put your best foot forward

Throughout this entire process, you may feel that the board individually and collectively is trying to pierce your defenses, seek out your hidden weaknesses and embarrass and confuse you. Actually, this is not true. They are obliged to make an appraisal of your qualifications for the job you are seeking, and they want to see you in your best light. Remember, they must interview all candidates and a non-cooperative candidate may become a failure in spite of their best efforts to bring out his qualifications. Here are 15 suggestions that will help you:

1) Be natural – Keep your attitude confident, not cocky

If you are not confident that you can do the job, do not expect the board to be. Do not apologize for your weaknesses, try to bring out your strong points. The board is interested in a positive, not negative, presentation. Cockiness will antagonize any board member and make him wonder if you are covering up a weakness by a false show of strength.

2) Get comfortable, but don't lounge or sprawl

Sit erectly but not stiffly. A careless posture may lead the board to conclude that you are careless in other things, or at least that you are not impressed by the importance of the occasion. Either conclusion is natural, even if incorrect. Do not fuss with your clothing, a pencil or an ashtray. Your hands may occasionally be useful to emphasize a point; do not let them become a point of distraction.

3) Do not wisecrack or make small talk

This is a serious situation, and your attitude should show that you consider it as such. Further, the time of the board is limited – they do not want to waste it, and neither should you.

4) Do not exaggerate your experience or abilities

In the first place, from information in the application or other interviews and sources, the board may know more about you than you think. Secondly, you probably will not get away with it. An experienced board is rather adept at spotting such a situation, so do not take the chance.

5) If you know a board member, do not make a point of it, yet do not hide it

Certainly you are not fooling him, and probably not the other members of the board. Do not try to take advantage of your acquaintanceship – it will probably do you little good.

6) Do not dominate the interview

Let the board do that. They will give you the clues – do not assume that you have to do all the talking. Realize that the board has a number of questions to ask you, and do not try to take up all the interview time by showing off your extensive knowledge of the answer to the first one.

7) Be attentive

You only have 20 minutes or so, and you should keep your attention at its sharpest throughout. When a member is addressing a problem or question to you, give him your undivided attention. Address your reply principally to him, but do not exclude the other board members.

8) Do not interrupt

A board member may be stating a problem for you to analyze. He will ask you a question when the time comes. Let him state the problem, and wait for the question.

9) Make sure you understand the question

Do not try to answer until you are sure what the question is. If it is not clear, restate it in your own words or ask the board member to clarify it for you. However, do not haggle about minor elements.

10) Reply promptly but not hastily

A common entry on oral board rating sheets is "candidate responded readily," or "candidate hesitated in replies." Respond as promptly and quickly as you can, but do not jump to a hasty, ill-considered answer.

11) Do not be peremptory in your answers

A brief answer is proper – but do not fire your answer back. That is a losing game from your point of view. The board member can probably ask questions much faster than you can answer them.

12) Do not try to create the answer you think the board member wants

He is interested in what kind of mind you have and how it works – not in playing games. Furthermore, he can usually spot this practice and will actually grade you down on it.

13) Do not switch sides in your reply merely to agree with a board member

Frequently, a member will take a contrary position merely to draw you out and to see if you are willing and able to defend your point of view. Do not start a debate, yet do not surrender a good position. If a position is worth taking, it is worth defending.

14) Do not be afraid to admit an error in judgment if you are shown to be wrong

The board knows that you are forced to reply without any opportunity for careful consideration. Your answer may be demonstrably wrong. If so, admit it and get on with the interview.

15) Do not dwell at length on your present job

The opening question may relate to your present assignment. Answer the question but do not go into an extended discussion. You are being examined for a *new* job, not your present one. As a matter of fact, try to phrase ALL your answers in terms of the job for which you are being examined.

Basis of Rating

Probably you will forget most of these "do's" and "don'ts" when you walk into the oral interview room. Even remembering them all will not ensure you a passing grade. Perhaps you did not have the qualifications in the first place. But remembering them will help you to put your best foot forward, without treading on the toes of the board members.

Rumor and popular opinion to the contrary notwithstanding, an oral board wants you to make the best appearance possible. They know you are under pressure – but they also want to see how you respond to it as a guide to what your reaction would be under the pressures of the job you seek. They will be influenced by the degree of poise you display, the personal traits you show and the manner in which you respond.

EXAMINATION SECTION

EXAMINATION SECTION
TEST 1

DIRECTIONS: Each question or incomplete statement is followed by several suggested answers or completions. Select the one the BEST answers the question or completes the statement. *PRINT THE LETTER OF THE CORRECT ANSWER IN THE SPACE AT THE RIGHT.*

1. When formulating a puppy's diet, it is important to remember that a deficiency in _____ can cause rickets (bone deformities).   1.____

    A. iron
    B. vitamin A
    C. potassium
    D. vitamin D

2. Feeding raw meat to cats may increase the risk of transmitting   2.____

    A. toxoplasmosis
    B. coronavirus
    C. rabies
    D. panleukopenia

3. In general, dogs in a shelter should be exercised   3.____

    A. 15-20 minutes, once a day
    B. 10-15 minutes twice a day
    C. 30-40 minutes twice a day
    D. about 2 hours, once a day

4. If a disinfectant such as Chlorazon is used to clean part of the shelter facility,   4.____

    A. the solution should remain on the surface for at least 10 minutes
    B. don't allow the solution to soak too far below the surface or into cracks
    C. it should be mixed with another complementary cleaner such as a detergent
    D. the solution should be rinsed well before 5 minutes have passed

5. The type of dog least likely to tolerate having another animal housed above itand which therefore should always be housed in an upper tier when possibleis the   5.____

    A. border collie
    B. poodle
    C. terrier
    D. Labrador

6. A typical "old age" formula dog food should have a dry-matter fat content of about ' %.   6.____

    A. 3-10
    B. 10-15
    C. 15-30
    D. 20-30

7. Which of the following is <u>not</u> usually a sign that a dog is thinking of biting?   7.____

    A. A hard stare
    B. A slow turning of the head
    C. A tucked tail
    D. A stiffening posture

8. A new arrival at a shelter is a geriatric dog who experiences some difficulty lifting itself up   8.____
onto its back legs. The shelter has no food formulated for older dogs. Generally, if the
dog is given the same food as other adult dogs, each serving should be

    A. about 25% smaller than that of the other dogs
    B. diluted with about a cup of water
    C. about 40% larger than that of the other dogs
    D. ground into small pieces

9. Which of the following diseases are communicable from animals to humans?   9.____
    I. Chicken pox
    II. Diphtheria
    III. Tuberculosis
    IV. Coronavirus

    A. I and II
    B. I and IV
    C. II, III and IV
    D. I, II, III and IV

10. Probably the <u>least</u> desirable method of housing cats in a shelter is   10.____

    A. scattered-in pens randomly situated throughout, separated from each other by dog
       pens
    B. centrally-in adjacent pens, separate from dogs
    C. parallelin pens lined up in a row opposite the dog pens
    D. communally-together in a large building or a big room equipped with a variety of
       hideaways

11. A standard (14-oz) can of commercial adult-formula dog food will generally contain about   11.____
_____ kcal of energy.

    A. 100-200
    B. 300-400
    C. 500-600
    D. 600-800

12. Which of the following types of dogs is <u>least</u> predisposed toward demodectic or red   12.____
mange?

    A. Dachshund
    B. Doberman
    C. Cocker spaniel
    D. Pit bull terrier

13. When trimming the nails of a dog, it's useful to remember that the quick, which contains nerves and blood vessels, runs about _____ of the way down the nail.

    A. 1/8
    B. 1/4
    C. 1/2
    D. 3/4

13._____

14. Which of the following is <u>not</u> a common symptom or complication of feline leukemia?

    A. Diarrhea
    B. Abscesses
    C. Anemia
    D. Cancer

14._____

15. If cats need to be have pills administered, it's usually best to ease the pill into the cat's throat with

    A. forceps
    B. a cotton swab
    C. the eraser end of a pencil
    D. the middle finger

15._____

16. As a general rule, puppies should never be bathed until they have reached the age of

    A. 6 weeks
    B. 3 months
    C. 9 months
    D. 18 months

16._____

17. Which of the following temperatures (F) falls within the normal range for a cat?

    A. 103.2
    B. 101.7
    C. 98.8
    D. 96.9

17._____

18. Each of the following is a complication of hardpad in dogs, <u>except</u>

    A. convulsions
    B. chewing fits
    C. abdominal distress
    D. encephalitis

18._____

19. Just after an abscess is discovered on a cat, probably the best thing a caretaker can do is

    A. restrict the cat's water intake
    B. apply hot compresses to the abscess
    C. try to drain the abscess
    D. apply cold compresses to the abscess

19._____

20. Which of the following pests or parasites is most likely to be an intermediate carrier of tapeworms?

    A. Cockroaches
    B. Mosquitoes
    C. Fleas
    D. Ticks

20._____

21. A typical kitten formula food should have a dry-matter protein content of about _____ %.

    A. 10
    B. 20
    C. 30
    D. 40

21._____

22. Which of the following situations or signs of illness would necessitate an immediate, emergency visit to a veterinary clinic?

    A. Difficulty breathing
    B. Abnormal discharge from the eyes
    C. Lack of appetite
    D. Persistent vomiting or diarrhea

22._____

23. The onset of parvovirus is frequently indicated by each of the following, except

    A. vomiting
    B. anemia
    C. diarrhea
    D. fever

23._____

24. Minor flesh wounds on cats and dogs should ideally be flushed with a solution of

    A. 3% hydrogen peroxide
    B. 5% alcohol
    C. 10% iodine
    D. deionized, purified water

24._____

25. Which of the following is a water-soluble vitamin?

    A. A
    B. C
    C. E
    D. K

25._____

KEY (CORRECT ANSWERS)

1.	D		11.	C
2.	A		12.	C
3.	C		13.	D
4.	A		14.	A
5.	C		15.	C
6.	B		16.	B
7.	C		17.	B
8.	A		18.	C
9.	D		19.	B
10.	D		20.	C

21.	C
22.	A
23.	B
24.	A
25.	B

———

TEST 2

DIRECTIONS: Each question or incomplete statement is followed by several suggested answers or completions. Select the one the BEST answers the question or completes the statement. *PRINT THE LETTER OF THE CORRECT ANSWER IN THE SPACE AT THE RIGHT.*

1. Which of the following is the clearest sign that a new arrival to a shelter is adjusting well?   1.____

    A. Clawing or scratching to get out of cage or pen
    B. Moving from the back of the cage or pen to the front
    C. Relatively quiet demeanor
    D. Clean coat

2. The primary ingredient in most dry dog foods is   2.____

    A. bone meal
    B. cereal
    C. animal or poultry meat
    D. fat

3. For normal adult dogs and cats, which of the following is the best daily feeding proce-   3.____
dure?

    A. Serving four small portions a day
    B. Leaving the morning portion until it is consumed, and then following with an evening portion which is left until it is consumed
    C. Leaving two moderate portions, once early in the day and one later, and removing each after about 30 minutes or so.
    D. Leaving a large bowl of food, more than the animal needs, out all day long

4. Each of the following is an element of aggressive canine posture, <u>except</u>   4.____

    A. ears back
    B. eyes wide open
    C. head up
    D. tail flicking from side to side

5. One of the most important guidelines for the use of bacteria/enzyme cleaning solutions is   5.____
to

    A. apply them with an abrasive scrubber or brush
    B. use them only on surfaces that resist water damage
    C. leave them on the surface no longer than 1 minute
    D. use them in conjunction with a detergent or bleach solution

6. What is the term for a low level of calcium in a lactating female?   6.____

    A. hypocalcemia
    B. calcinosis
    C. lachrymosis
    D. eclampsia

7. A new arrival at a shelter has refused to eat for the last 18 hours.   7.____
    Which of the following is LEAST likely to make food more palatable to the animal?

    A. Warming the food
    B. Adding water
    C. Increasing the size of the portion
    D. Increasing the protein or fat content

8. Probably the best way to house cats in a shelter is   8.____

    A. scatteredin pens randomly situated throughout, separated from each other by dog pens
    B. centrally-in adjacent pens, separate from dogs
    C. parallelin pens lined up in a row opposite the dog pens
    D. communally-together in a large building or a big room equipped with a variety of hideaways

9. A new arrival at a shelter is being checked for obvious signs of sickness. After checking   9.____
    the head, the location most in need of attention is/are the

    A. anal/genital area
    B. belly between the hind legs
    C. chest
    D. paws

10. Which of the following is a symptom of leptospirosis?   10.____

    A. Coughing
    B. Excessive thirst
    C. Runny eyes
    D. Bleeding gums

11. When formulating a dog's diet, it is important to remember that the most toxic vitamin to   11.____
    dogs is

    A. A
    B. B
    C. D
    D. K

12. Indications of canine hepatitis include each of the following, except   12.____

    A. tonsillitis
    B. bleeding gums
    C. anemia
    D. loss of appetite

13. Which of the following pests or parasites has been linked to the spread of toxoplasmo-   13.____
    sis?

    A. Rats and mice
    B. Cockroaches
    C. Ticks
    D. Reas

14. A cat whose diet consists largely of canned tuna is at risk for   14.____

    A. tapeworm
    B. rickets
    C. vitamin A poisoning
    D. vitamin E deficiency

15. A cat's pulse can most easily and safely be found   15.____

    A. just behind the front paw
    B. in the neck
    C. just beneath an ear
    D. inside the hind leg where it joins the body

16. Generally, as a breed, which of the following types of cats should be expected to be LEAST cooperative in a shelter setting?   16.____

    A. Siamese
    B. American shorthair
    C. Russian blue
    D. Maine coon

17. A standard (14-oz) can of commercial adult-formula cat food will generally contain about _____ kcal of energy.   17.____

    A. 100-200
    B. 300-400
    C. 500-600
    D. 600-800

18. A typical adult formula cat food should have a dry-matter protein content of about _____ %.   18.____

    A. 15
    B. 25
    C. 35
    D. 45

19. Which of the following is one of the symptoms of canine distemper?   19.____

    A. Frequent urination
    B. Vomiting
    C. Respiratory distress
    D. Hard stool

20. Each of the following is a guideline to follow in bathing a cat or a dog, except   20.____

    A. part the hair of long-haired animals down the middle while bathing
    B. if the pet has a flea problem, lather around the tail first
    C. use lukewarm or room-temperature water
    D. wash the face and muzzle with a damp, soapy washcloth

21. A dog should see a veterinarian immediately if it is   21.____
    A. urinating with increasing frequency
    B. straining but unable to urinate
    C. passing a diminished flow of urine
    D. passing cloudy urine

22. A typical "old age" formula dog food should have a dry-matter protein content of about   22.____
    _____ %.

    A. 2-5
    B. 8-12
    C. 15-20
    D. 20-30

23. A dog has gradually lost weight over time, has a persistent cough, and has a reduced   23.____
    capacity for exercise. It should be checked as soon as possible for

    A. heartworm
    B. parvovirus
    C. leptospirosis
    D. whipwormt

24. Sarcoptic mange, or scabies,   24.____
    A. is highly contagious to other dogs
    B. first presents as bald spots
    C. does not cause itching
    D. cannot be transmitted to human beings

25. When a cat must be force-fed solid food, the food should be placed   25.____
    A. on the palate right behind the upper front teeth
    B. underneath the tongue
    C. in the back of the throat
    D. between the cheek pouch and the lower back teeth

KEY (CORRECT ANSWERS)

1.	B		11.	C
2.	B		12.	B
3.	C		13.	B
4.	A		14.	D
5.	B		15.	D
6.	D		16.	A
7.	C		17.	B
8.	A		18.	B
9.	A		19.	C
10.	D		20.	B

21.	B
22.	C
23.	A
24.	A
25.	A

———

EXAMINATION SECTION
TEST 1

DIRECTIONS: Each question or incomplete statement is followed by several suggested answers or completions. Select the one the BEST answers the question or completes the statement. *PRINT THE LETTER OF THE CORRECT ANSWER IN THE SPACE AT THE RIGHT.*

1. For normal adult dogs and cats, which of the following is the best daily watering procedure?   1.____

    A. Making fresh, clean water available 24 hours a day.
    B. Leaving a water dish with the food dish, and removing the water dish after the food has been consumed.
    C. Leaving a water dish twice a day for about 30 minutes each time.
    D. Watering once in the morning, for as long as the animal drinks.

2. When dealing with problem dogs in a shelter—either aggressive or overly anxious—it's important to remember that the dog's need for _____ will usually override most other concerns when it comes to behavior.   2.____

    A. canine companionship
    B. food and water
    C. open space and exercise
    D. human approval

3. Each of the following is an advantage associated with the use of dry foods for animals in a shelter over wet or canned foods, except   3.____

    A. low cost
    B. slower rate of spoilage
    C. fewer dental problems
    D. higher energy content

4. A dog that is fed an all-meat diet is at risk for seizure-like tremors hat are caused by a deficiency in   4.____

    A. vitamin K   B. calcium   C. phosphorus   D. vitamin E

5. The biggest drawback to confining cats communally in a shelter is   5.____

    A. unwanted pregnancy
    B. the increased likelihood of injury
    C. the poor socialization of cats with humans, decreasing their chance of adoption
    D. the fact that some cats disappear upon introduction and are rarely seen

6. If a cat is to undergo a scheduled diet change, the change should take place   6.____

    A. immediately and conspicuously
    B. immediately, but without the cat noticing, if possible
    C. gradually over a period of 5-10 days
    D. gradually over a period of 15-30 days

7. Typically, an abscess on a cat can be resolved in one of several ways. Which of the following is <u>not</u> usually recommended?   7.____

    A. Giving moderate antibiotic doses
    B. Leaving the abscess alone and allowing the body to carry away the toxins
    C. Lancing the abscess and making sure it doesn't close up again
    D. Allowing the abscess to burst and discharge the pus, and men heal as any wound would

8. When laying out litter trays for cats, it's usually a good idea to use _____ in each tray.   8.____

    A. little more than an inch or so of clay
    B. about six inches of clay
    C. more than an inch of sand
    D. a 3 to 6-inch deep sand/clay mixture

9. No matter how dirty it gets, a dog should never be washed more frequently than   9.____

    A. once a day
    B. twice a week
    C. once a week
    D. once a month

10. When giving liquid medication to a cat, one should typically   10.____

    A. try to deliver it all in one squirt
    B. insert the dropper into the corner of the mouth
    C. aim the dropper at the back of the throat
    D. simply put the medicine in a small amount of water and let the cat drink it voluntarily

11. Which of the following is <u>not</u> a common symptom of canine hepatitis?   11.____

    A. Trembling
    B. Fluctuating fever
    C. Runny nose
    D. Loss of appetite

12. Each of the following diseases is communicable from animals to humans, <u>except</u>   12.____

    A. heartworm
    B. mumps
    C. parvovirus
    D. scarlet fever

13. When a commercial feline milk-replacement is not available for a kitten, an emergency substitute can be made that should include each of the following, <u>except:</u>   13.____

    A. skim milk
    B. mayonnaise
    C. active-culture yogurt
    D. water

14. A dog has refused to eat for several days, despite repeated attempts to make the food more palatable and the animal more comfortable. A veterinary examination reveals no medical problem. The animal should be

14.____

    A. undergo a vigorous exercise routine to stimulate its appetite
    B. force-fed with a syringe or baster
    C. fed intravenously
    D. left alone until it begins eating on its own

15. A dog begins scratching uncontrollably. Closer examination reveals small round, hairless areas. Most likely, the dog has a case of

15.____

    A. sarcoptic mange (scabies)
    B. demodectic (red) mange
    C. round worm
    D. hookworm

16. An Elizabethan collar is useful for dogs experiencing each of the following conditions, <u>except</u>

16.____

    A. pseudopregnancy
    B. keratitis
    C. corneal dystrophy
    D. post-surgery

17. A typical "maintenance" formula dog food should have a dry-matter protein content of about _____ %.

17.____

    A. 8-15
    B. 15-35
    C. 25-40
    D. 35-55

18. The most complete method of odor control in or on a porous surface is to apply

18.____

    A. a 2% ammonia solution
    B. a 2% bleach solution
    C. a combination bleach/detergent solution
    D. a combination bacteria/enzyme digester

19. A cat has a swollen paw. The most likely cause is

19.____

    A. rubber band or twine around paw
    B. an abscess under the skin
    C. an infection of the claw
    D. arthritis

20. The signs of anaphylactic shock in a cat include

20.____

    A. trembling
    B. discharge from the eyes
    C. high temperature
    D. sudden diarrhea

21. Systemic flea killers

    A. kill flea eggs
    B. are useful after a serious infestation is under way
    C. begin to work only after a flea has bitten the animal
    D. have no known side effects

21.___

22. If a cat is observed to frequently shake its head violently, it is most likely a sign of

    A. brucellosis
    B. ear mites
    C. idiopathic epilepsy
    D. ticks

22.___

23. A dog in a shelter has begun to gag and occasionally regurgitate yellow bile, and it passes smelly, mucous-coated stools. This is most likely a sign of

    A. coronavirus
    B. leptospirosis
    C. parvovirus
    D. hardpad

23.___

24. Which of the following pests or parasites is most likely to be a carrier of heartworm?

    A. Biting flies
    B. Mosquitoes
    C. Fleas
    D. Ticks

24.___

25. When lifting a large dog, one hand should be

    A. around the neck, and the other hand under the abdomen
    B. under the muzzle, and the other under the abdomen
    C. around the shoulder muscles, and the other around the hind leg muscles
    D. around the chest, and the other hand around the abdomen

25.___

KEY (CORRECT ANSWERS)

1.	A	11.	C
2.	D	12.	C
3.	D	13.	A
4.	B	14.	B
5.	D	15.	C
6.	C	16.	C
7.	A	17.	B
8.	A	18.	D
9.	C	19.	B
10.	B	20.	D

21. C
22. B
23. A
24. B
25. C

TEST 2

DIRECTIONS: Each question or incomplete statement is followed by several suggested answers or completions. Select the one the BEST answers the question or completes the statement. *PRINT THE LETTER OF THE CORRECT ANSWER IN THE SPACE AT THE RIGHT.*

1. When maintaining a shelter, it's important to remember that cats are highly sensitive to many chemical products, and should not come into contact with most cleaners customarily used for dogs. In particular, it's important to keep cats away from products containing _____ or its by-products.   1.____

   A. sodium hydroxide
   B. sodium hypochlorite
   C. phenol
   D. ammonia

2. A middle-sized dog, a new arrival at a shelter, needs to be removed from a pen so that it can be cleaned. The dog is nervous, however, and settles back into a corner to avoid having to leave. If it cannot be coaxed, the best way to extricate it from the pen is to   2.____

   A. send an accomplice around back to startle the dog out
   B. reach in to pet and comfort it until it relents
   C. withhold food until it can be lured out by its own hunger
   D. fasten a loop or leash and pull the dog gently out until it can be scooped up

3. The most likely result of a sudden dietary change—for either a cat or a dog—is   3.____

   A. constipation
   B. fever
   C. diarrhea
   D. vomiting

4. With problem dogs, it is best to approach their handling and care with a _____ attitude.   4.____

   A. domineering and intimidating
   B. tender and affectionate
   C. indifferent
   D. firm and businesslike

5. The signs of early shock in a cat include   5.____

   A. pale gums
   B. irregular heartbeat
   C. extreme weakness
   D. unconsciousness

6. A dry adult-formula dog food will generally contain about _____ kcal of energy per 1 cup.   6.____

   A. 100-200
   B. 300-400
   C. 500-600
   D. 600-800

7. A cat's level of hydration can be most easily assessed by   7.____

    A. close observation of urinary patterns
    B. checking the coloration of the eyes
    C. close observation of drinking
    D. pinching the skin on the neck

8. A cat's resting heart rate typically varies from _____ beats per minute.   8.____

    A. 30-40
    B. 75-100
    C. 110-160
    D. 180-240

9. A cat complains loudly whenever it is touched, on virtually any part of its body. The most   9.____
    likely cause is

    A. vitamin A deficiency
    B. old age
    C. gastrointestinal upset
    D. a case of steatitis

10. Toxic reactionsto pesticides or other poisonscommonly include each of the following   10.____
    symptoms in cats and dogs, except

    A. depression
    B. rapid or shallow breathing
    C. frequent urination
    D. convulsions

11. A dog may be at risk for vitamin _____ toxicity if it is fed a diet too rich in liver.   11.____

    A. A
    B. D
    C. E
    D. K

12. For both dogs and cats, a diet that is deficient in salt (sodium chloride) is likely to result in   12.____
    either of the following symptoms, except

    A. fatigue
    B. hair loss
    C. bleeding gums
    D. poor growth

13. Which of the following statements is true of demodectic or red mange?   13.____

    A. It is highly contagious
    B. Older dogs are most frequently afflicted
    C. The affected area is usually itchy
    D. It is often attributed to stress

14. A cat's temperature is 106° F. The caretaker should   14.____
    A. keep the cat warm and seek immediate veterinary attention
    B. do nothing—it's a normal temperature
    C. keep an eye on the cat and seek veterinary attention within 24 hours
    D. cool the cat down and seek immediate veterinary attention

15. Which of the following should not be part of one's approach in the feeding regimen of an   15.____
    aging cat?
    A. Large amounts of vitamin supplements with meals
    B. Supplying additional enzymes
    C. Large amounts of protein supplements with meals
    D. Feeding smaller meals more frequently

16. Which of the following is recommended for the control of parvovirus and coronavirus in   16.____
    kennels, runs and pens?
    A. 2% bleach solution
    B. 5% ammonia solution
    C. 5% alcohol solution
    D. 10% hydrogen peroxide solution

17. A cat has a dull coat and appears to have lost weight. Occasionally, the cat vomits,   17.____
    despite no recent changes in diet. Which of the following conditions is most likely?
    A. Roundworm
    B. Brucellosis
    C. Tapeworm
    D. Coronavirus

18. Which of the following should never be used to clean up animal urine?   18.____
    A. Bleach
    B. Detergent
    C. Ammonia
    D. Enzyme solution

19. Moist food that has been left for an animal should be discarded no later than _____   19.____
    later.
    A. 1 hour
    B. 4 hours
    C. 12 hours
    D. 24 hours

20. Which of the following situations or signs of illness is a problem worthy of veterinary con-   20.____
    sultation on a non-emergency basis?
    A. Collapse
    B. Exposure to extreme hot or cold
    C. Abnormal swelling
    D. Hemorrhage

21. A dog is overweight. Overall, the dietary goal for the animal should be to reduce its caloric intake to _____ % of the requirement for its estimated ideal weight.

    A. 25-35
    B. 40-50
    C. 60-70
    D. 80-90

21.____

22. A shelter runs out of cat food, and maintains its cats on dog food or a while. This practice can lead to a deficiency of _____ in the cats' diet.

    A. antioxidants
    B. soluble fiber
    C. crude protein
    D. the amino acid taurine

22.____

23. A distended abdomen may be a sign that an animal is infested with

    A. heartworm
    B. hookworm
    C. tapeworm
    D. whipworm

23.____

24. When trimming the nails of a cat, one should stay at least _____ inch away from the quick, which contains nerves and blood vessels.

    A. 1/8
    B. 1/4
    C. 1/2
    D. 3/4

24.____

25. A cat will need to be force-fed because it is suffering from an illness that has taken away its appetite. Which of the following will increase the chances that the cat will accept the food?

    A. Giving saline nose drops five minutes before mealtime
    B. Giving an enema ten minutes before
    C. Withholding water for 12 hours before
    D. Refrigerating the food

25.____

KEY (CORRECT ANSWERS)

1.	C		11.	A
2.	D		12.	C
3.	C		13.	D
4.	D		14.	D
5.	A		15.	C
6.	B		16.	A
7.	D		17.	A
8.	C		18.	C
9.	D		19.	A
10.	C		20.	C

21.	C
22.	D
23.	C
24.	B
25.	A

———

EXAMINATION SECTION

DIRECTIONS: Each question or incomplete statement is followed by several suggested answers or completions. Select the one that BEST answers the question or completes the statement. *PRINT THE LETTER OF THE CORRECT ANSWER IN THE SPACE AT THE RIGHT.*

1. The dark-shaded portion of the dog's coat on the shoulders, back, and sides is called the
   A. mantle   B. mane   C. mask   D. apron   E. blanket

   1. ___

2. The dark shading of the dog's foreface is called the
   A. crown   B. culotte   C. beard   D. mask   E. thumb marks

   2. ___

3. The longer fringe of hair on the dog's ears, legs, tail, or body is called
   A. fall   B. feathering   C. saddle   D. plume   E. pile

   3. ___

4. A Collie's longer hair below the neck on the chest is called the
   A. frill   B. feathering   C. apron   D. blaze   E. bloom

   4. ___

5. Height is measured from the dog's
   A. ears   B. head   C. tail   D. shoulders   E. back

   5. ___

6. What is a cryptorchid?   A
   A. castrated male dog   B. neutered female dog
   C. male dog with both testicles descended into the scrotum
   D. male dog who has sired puppies
   E. male dog whose testicles have not descended into the scrotum

   6. ___

7. A female dog normally has her *first* heat-cycle
   A. at three months of age
   B. between three and six months of age
   C. between seven and twelve months of age
   D. at one year of age
   E. after the age of one year

   7. ___

8. From weaning to six weeks of age, puppies should be fed
   A. as often as they will eat   B. once a day
   C. twice a day   D. four times a day
   E. only by the mother

   8. ___

9. A well-balanced diet for an adult dog should consist of
   A. meat   B. cereal and bones
   C. cereal, proteins, and minerals
   D. meat and one raw-egg white daily
   E. cereal and table scraps

   9. ___

10. Bones are 10. __
    A. *beneficial* because they help keep a dog's teeth clean
    B. *beneficial* because they massage a dog's gums
    C. *beneficial* as a food supplement
    D. *harmful* because they can break and splinter, causing injury
    E. *harmful* because the dog will lose his taste for dog food

11. The *best* way to rid a dog of ticks is to 11. __
    A. kill them with the tip of a lighted cigarette
    B. remove them with tweezers
    C. kill them with kerosene or gasoline
    D. submerge the dog in a bath of warm water for fiteeen
       minutes
    E. apply any household or garden insecticide

12. The *best* time to start training a puppy is 12. __
    A. the day you bring him home
    B. when he misbehaves
    C. when he is housebroken
    D. when he is six months of age
    E. not before he is one—year old

13. To correct a puppy for his mistakes, you should 13. __
    A. never correct a puppy because he is too young to understand
    B. wait until he is thoroughly familiar with his new home
    C. correct him immediately when he misbehaves
    D. always make him come to you first so that he understands
       who is the boss
    E. drag him to the "scene of the crime" so, that he will un-
       derstand his mistake

14. The *best* way to tell whether a dog has a fever is to 14. __
    A. feel whether his nose is cold
    B. feel whether his nose is hot
    C. feel whether his coat is warm
    D. take his temperature with an oral thermometer
    E. take his temperature with a rectal thermometer

15. In administering first aid to a dog, the *first* thing you 15. __
    should do is to
    A. tie his mouth shut   B. take his temperature
    C. determine the extent of his injuries
    D. take him to a veterinarian
    E. keep him warm

16. Mating very closely-related dogs such as mother and son or 16. __
    brother and sister is called
    A. cross breeding   B. in-breeding
    C. line breeding   D. mixed breeding
    E. out-breeding

17. A bitch is 17. __
    A. any female dog   B. only a female dog in heat
    C. only a neutered female dog
    D. only a pregnant female dog
    E. only a female dog who has had puppies

18. The *average* gestation period for a dog is   18. ____
    A. twenty-one days   B. thirty-six days
    C. sixty-three days   D. six months
    E. nine months

19. A suitable method to induce vomiting in a dog is to   19. ____
    A. give him warm milk
    B. give him warm water
    C. give him a tiny bit of poison in water
    D. give him equal parts of hydrogen peroxide and water
    E. immediately immobolize his tongue with your fingers

20. Eclampsia is an insufficient amount of   20. ____
    A. milk   B. calcium   C. protein   D. phosphorus
    E. potassium

21. Mastitis refers to   21. ____
    A. the removal of the mammary glands
    B. a malignant breast tumor
    C. a benign breast tumor
    D. an inability to lactate
    E. an inflammation of the nursing dam's teats

22. *Which* of the following is *true* of a Guide Dog?   22. ____
    A. Only male dogs are used
    B. Only female dogs are used
    C. Only altered male or female dogs are used
    D. Any male or female dog can be used
    E. Only "Working Class" dogs can be used

23. Puppies should be weaned   23. ____
    A. as soon as they are whelped
    B. when the mother's milk supply is insufficient
    C. at three weeks of age
    D. at three months of age
    E. just before they are going to be removed from the mother

24. The only dog breed with a blue-black tongue is the   24. ____
    A. Pekinese   B. Pug   C. Shih-Tzu
    D. Chinese Fighting Dog   E. Chow Chow

25. This dog is called the "Monkey Dog" because of its monkeyish 25. ____
    facial expression, bushy eyebrows, and striking black eyes.
    This breed is the
    A. Pomerian   B. Affenpinscher   C. Brussel Griffon
    D. Puli   E. Briand

26. The Bearded Collie *most closely* resembles the   26. ____
    A. Puli   B. Belgian Sheepdog   C. Border Collie
    D. Rough Collie   E. Smooth Collie

27. The *only* breed of dog that *does not* bark is the   27. ____
    A. Australian Kelpie   B. Lakeland Terrier
    C. Alaskan Malamute   D. Basenji   E. Chow Chow

3

28. *Accepted* coat colors for the Doberman Pinscher include all   28. __
    of the following EXCEPT
       A. black   B. red   C. brown   D. blue   E. fawn

29. A pure-white coat marked with small, distinct dark brown   29. __
    or black spots, is the *chief* characteristic of the
       A. American Staffordshire Terrier   B. Bluetick Coonhound
       C. Borzoi   D. Dalmatian   E. Catahoula Leopard Dog

30. White, long, thick hair that develops into heavy tassel-like   30. __
    cords is the *chief* characteristic of the
       A. Afghan Hound   B. Bichon Frise   C. Briand
       D. Lhasa Apsos   E. Komondor

31. The Russian Wolfhound is *today* called the   31. __
       A. Basenji   B. Borzoi   C. Saluki   D. Great Pyrenees
       E. Rottweiler

32. A strong swimmer with webbed feet and able to withstand icy   32. __
    waters describes the
       A. Newfoundland   B. Chesapeake Bay Retriever
       C. American Water Spaniel   D. Brittany Spaniel
       E. Flat-coated Retriever

33. A dog with a distinctive lamb-like appearance is the   33. __
    _____ Terrier.
       A. Lakeland   B. Dandie Dinmont   C. Australian
       D. Bedlington   E. Sealyham

34. All of the following are distinct Retriever breeds EXCEPT the   34. __
    _____ Retriever.
       A. Wire-haired   B. Curyl-coated   C. Flat-coated
       D. Golden   E. Labrador

35. A flat, silky mahogany or rich chestnut red coat is the   35. __
    chief characteristic of the
       A. Gordon Setter   B. Irish Setter   C. English Setter
       D. English Cocker Spaniel   E. Cocker Spaniel

36. Except for size, the Harrier is the external replica of the   36. __
       A. American Foxhound   B. Basenji   C. Beagle
       D. Basset Hound   E. English Foxhound

37. The *fastest* domesticated animal of his weight, capable of   37. __
    speeds up to thirty-five miles per hour, is the
       A. Scottish Deerhound   B. Saluki   C. Whippet
       D. Italian Greyhound   E. Greyhound

38. Bachsunds may be all of the following EXCEPT   38. __
       A. short-haired (smooth-coat)   B. wire-haired
       C. long-haired   D. curly-haired   E. miniature

39. Great Danes may have all of the following coat colors EXCEPT   39. __
       A. brindle   B. fawn   C. white   D. black   E. harlequin

40. A short, smooth coat of sleek mouse-gray to silver-gray color   40. __
    is the *chief* characteristic of the
       A. Greyhound   B. Pharoah Hound   C. Bullmastiff
       D. Basenji   E. Weimaraner

4

41. The *best* way to break a dog of a bad habit is to   41. ___
    A. exercise eternal vigilance and apply immediate correction
    B. soundly spank him
    C. withhold food
    D. lock him in a small, dark area such as a closet
    E. keep him outdoors until he learns how to behave in the
       house

42. A dog's ears may be *safely* cleaned with a cotton ball   42. ___
    moistened with
    A. soap and water   B. baby oil   C. alcohol
    D. peroxide   E. baking soda and water

43. If a puppy has not opened his eyes in ten to fifteen days,   43. ___
    A. gently pry the lids open
    B. applu warm compresses to the lids
    C. seek veterinary advice
    D. induce the female to lick the eyelids open
    E. don't worry because some breeds take longer than others

44. A dog's nails should be clipped   44. ___
    A. only by a veterinarian
    B. once a year
    C. only if the dog is inactive
    D. periodically so the nails just clear the floor
    E. only if the standard of the breed requires it

45. The *best* way to house break a puppy is to   45. ___
    A. keep the puppy outdoors until he develops control
    B. keep the puppy confined to a small sleeping area
    C. accustom the puppy to the entire house and be ready to
       rish him outdoors
    D. keep him tied on a short leash
    E. keep newspapers a good distance form his bed

46. All of the following have a characteristic pure-white coat   46. ___
    EXCEPT the
    A. Kuvasz   B. Maltese   C. Komondor
    D. West Highland White Terrier   E. Iceland Dog

47. The *best* method to administer capsule medication is to   47. ___
    A. place the capsule under the dog's tongue
    B. place the capsule on the tip of the dog's tongue
    C. place the capsule in the back of the dog's throat
    D. place the capsule in the funnel-like pouch formed by
       pulling out the dog's bottom lip
    E. empty the capsule's powder into the dog's food

48. A *good* rule to follow with regard to bathing a dog is: 48. ___
    A. A dog should never be bathed
    B. Bathe the dog twice a year
    C. Bathe the dog once a year
    D. Bathe the dog only if he is extremely dirty and odorous
    E. Bathe the dog only if he likes the water

49. A unique ridge of hair that runs the length of the back is   49. ___
    the *chief* characteristic of the
    A. Rhodesian Ridgeback   B. Otter Hound   C. Rottweiler
    D. Puli   E. Akita

5

50. All of the following are *good* guidelines in obedience   50. ___
    training EXCEPT:
    A. Always use the same vocabulary
    B. Always work for only short time-periods
    C. Always work in the same location
    D. Always act pleased and encouraging
    E. Always work before a pleasurable activity such as
       eating or playing

KEY (CORRECT ANSWERS)

1.	A	11.	B	21.	E	31.	B	41.	A
2.	D	12.	A	22.	C	32.	A	42.	B
3.	B	13.	C	23.	C	33.	D	43.	C
4.	C	14.	E	24.	E	34.	A	44.	D
5.	D	15.	A	25.	B	35.	B	45.	B
6.	E	16.	B	26.	A	36.	E	46.	E
7.	C	17.	A	27.	D	37.	C	47.	C
8.	D	18.	C	28.	C	38.	D	48.	D
9.	C	19.	D	29.	D	39.	C	49.	A
10.	D	20.	B	30.	E	40.	E	50.	C

EXAMINATION SECTION

DIRECTIONS: Each question or incomplete statement is followed by several suggested answers or completions. Select the one that BEST answers the question or completes the statement. *PRINT THE LETTER OF THE CORRECT ANSWER IN THE SPACE AT THE RIGHT.*

1. Conception is *most likely* if the female is mated   1. ____
   A. at the first sign of her heat cycle
   B. at the first appearance of a discharge
   C. during the first week of the heat cycle
   D. during the tenth to the fourteenth day of her heat cycle
   E. during the eighteenth to the twenty-first day of her heat cycle

2. All of the following are signs that a female is close to   2. ____
   whelping EXCEPT: She
   A. pants and breathes heavily
   B. looks anxiously at her rear quarters
   C. frequently urinates
   D. refuses food
   E. exhibits extreme restlessness

3. During whelping,   3. ____
   A. always remain a good distance from the female
   B. keep her alone in a dimly-lit room
   C. prevent her from eating the placenta
   D. keep a bowl of hot water nearby
   E. stay with her and be prepared to give assistance

4. The *largest* of the terrier family is the _____ Terrier.   4. ____
   A. Airedale   B. American Staffordshire
   C. Cairn   D. Lakeland   E. Scottish

5. A dog with a very wiry coat and a characteristic "otter-   5. ____
   like" head describes the _____ Terrier.
   A. Cairn   B. Bull   C. Irish   D. Skye
   E. Border

6. A toy dog covered from head to foot with a characteristic   6. ____
   mantle of silky, white hair describes the
   A. Shih Tzu   B. Pekinese   C. Maltese
   D. Silky Terrier   E. Yorkshire Terrier

7. The *largest* and *tallest* of the galloping hounds is the   7. ____
   A. Afghan Hound   B. Black and Tan Coonhound
   C. Irish Wolfhound   D. Basenji
   E. American Foxhound

8. An exotic expression, a long silky topnot, very prominent   8. ____
   hip bones, and thick, silky hair describes the
   A. Borzoi   B. Saluki   C. Otter Hound
   D. Afghan Hound E. Long-haired Dachshund

9. A short-legged dog, heavier in bone for its size than any   9. ___
   other breed, describes the
      A. Beagle   B. Dachshund   C. Sealyham Terrier
      D. Sussex Spaniel   E. Basset Hound

10. The skin is thin to the touch and extremely loose, especial-   10. ___
    ly about the head and neck where it hangs in deep folds,
    describes the
      A. Bloodhound   B. St. Bernard   C. Black and Tan Coonhound
      D. Vizsla   E. Manchester Terrier

11. An extremely hardy hunting dog with a distinctive dense   11. ___
    gray coat is the
      A. Irish Wolfhound   B. Otter Hound
      C. Rhodesian Ridgeback   D. Scottish Deerhound
      E. Norwegian Elkhound

12. A dog that hunts on both land and water with a rough double   12. ___
    coat and webbed feet describes the
      A. Black and Tan Coonhound   B. Otter Hound   C. Basenji
      D. Bloodhound   E. English Foxhound

13. African Lion Hound is another name for the   13. ___
      A. Rhodesian Ridgeback   B. Chow Chow   C. Akita
      D. Bichon Frise   E. Ibizan Hound

14. The royal dog of Egypt, bred for speed and endurance to   14. ___
    kill quarry over deep sand and rocky mountains, is the
      A. Schipperke   B. Samoyed   C. Vizsla
      D. Puli   E. Saluki

15. Distinguished by a grayish-white face with either cap-like   15. ___
    or mask-like markings and "snowshoe"-type feet aptly describes
    the
      A. Samoyed   B. Great Pyrenees   C. Akita
      D. Alaskan Malamute   E. Bernese Mountain Dog

16. A tog dog, distinguished by beautiful, erect butterfly-like   16. ___
    ears, is the
      A. Papillon   B. Shih-tzu   C. Pomeranian
      D. Yorkshire Terrier   E. Japanese Spaniel

17. The *best* way to administer liquid medicine is to pour it   17. ___
      A. down the back of the dog's throat
      B. under his tongue
      C. into his water bowl
      D. on the wide, flat part of the tongue
      E. into the funnel-like pounch of the bottom lip

18. All of the following are used in sled-work *except* the   18. ___
      A. Kuvasz   B. Great Pyrenees   C. Alaskan Malamute
      D. Samoyed   E. Siberian Husky

19. Stripping is a term signifying removal of
   A. matted hair   B. dead hair   C. all hair
   D. some hair for appearance   E. tangled hair

19. ____

20. A hound glove is used to
   A. give a hunting dog the scent
   B. handle game
   C. polish the coat of short-haired dogs
   D. separate tangles of long-haired dogs
   E. shape thick, curly-coated hair

20. ____

21. Pure-bred puppies are produced by all of the following EXCEPT:
   A. Any mating between identical dogs of the same breed
   B. Out-breeding
   C. Cross-breeding
   D. Line-breeding
   E. In-breeding

21. ____

22. The *best* time to mate a female for the *first* time is _____ of age.
   A. at six months   B. one year   C. eighteen months
   D. three years   E. five years

22. ____

23. If a puppy has not begun to breathe after birth,
   A. place the puppy on the mother's nipple
   B. keep the puppy warm
   C. clear the puppy's mouth of mucus
   D. follow the rules for artificial respiration
   E. there is nothing that can be done

23. ____

24. *How many* teeth does an adult dog have?
   A. Twenty   B. Twenty-two   C. Thirty-two
   D. Thirty-six E. Forty-two

24. ____

25. The *first* secretion in the female's nipples essential to new-born puppies is
   A. lactogen   B. colostrum   C. proestrum
   D. anestrum   E. metestrum

25. ____

26. The *average* length of the female heat cycle is
   A. one week   B. ten days   C. twenty-one days
   D. one month   E. six months

26. ____

27. All of the following are true of new-born puppies EXCEPT: They
   A. cannot see   B. do not have the instinct for elimination
   C. are born without hair   D. are born without teeth
   E. cannot hear

27. ____

28. A pregnant female needs *more*
   A. egg whites   B. yeast   C. mulk and meat
   D. milk and oil   E. salt

28. ____

29. A puppy does not completely control his bladder and anus until he is
   A. weaned   B. removed from the mother
   C. eight weeks old   D. four months old   E. six months old

29. ____

3

30. Sarcoptic mange mites cause a disease called   30. ____
    A. bubonic plague   B. scabies   C. coccidiosis
    D. leptospirosis   E. acne

31. Severe anemia can be caused by   31. ____
    A. fleas   B. whipworms   C. mites
    D. hookworms   E. tapeworms

32. The larvae of tapeworms is carried by   32. ____
    A. flies   B. mosquitoes   C. ticks
    D. mites   E. fleas

33. Heartworm is transmitted directly to the dog by an infected   33. ____
    A. tick   B. mosquito   C. mite   D. rat   E. fly

34. A human should not let his skin come into contact with a   34. ____
    dog infected with
    A. ringworm   B. tapeworm   C. eczema
    D. whip   E. heartworm

35. Leptospirosis is a dangerous disease because of the damage   35. ____
    it does to the
    A. liver   B. heart   C. kidneys   D. nervous system
    E. reproductive organs

36. Leptospirosis is a bacterial disease carried by   36. ____
    A. ticks   B. lice   C. flies   D. mosquitoes
    E. rats

37. The normal body temperature of a dog is   37. ____
    A. 96.8° B. 101.5° C. 98.6° D. 99.2° E. 103°

38. The *first* symptom of progressive retinal atrophy is   38. ____
    A. opacity of the lens   B. corneal opacity
    C. inturned lids   D. night blindness
    E. excessive blinking

39. The viral disease that can infect *both* humans and dogs is   39. ____
    A. canine herpesvirus   B. canine infectious hepatitis
    C. distemper   D. canine tracheobronchitis
    E. rabies

40. Brandy is useful   40. ____
    A. to calm a dog involved in an accident
    B. after a heart attack
    C. to warm an older dog
    D. after a fainting spell
    E. after a fit

41. All of the following are reasons why you should *not* attempt   41. ____
    to worm a dog with a commercial medication EXCEPT:
    A. Worms may not be the trouble and indiscriminate worming
       will do further harm
    B. A normal dose given to a sick or run-down dog may be
       lethal
    C. The type of worm must be identified for the treatment to
       be effective
    D. When the worms are not killed but only stunned enough to be
       passed out in the stool, they endanger other animals
    E. Some dogs require preliminary measures such as blood
       transfusions before worming is begun

42. An *important* point to remember in beginning a heartworm prevention program is
    A. to begin after the last frost in spring and continue through to the first frost of autumn
    B. to make certain through a blood test that the dog is not already infected with heartworm
    C. that the dog must have a transfusion before treatment is begun
    D. to give the dog an enema to clear the intestines of other internal parasites
    E. to make certain through microscoptic examination of a stool sample that the dog is not already infected with heartworm

42. ___

43. Luxation of the matella or dislocation of the knee cap is *more common*
    A. in hunting dogs   B. among racing dogs
    C. in larger breeds   D. in miniature and toy dogs
    E. among older dogs

43. ___

44. Distemper virus is *most commonly* spread by
    A. contact with an infected dog's saliva
    B. inhalation of infected air
    C. contact with an infected dog's stool
    D. drinking infected water
    E. contact with an infected dog's urine

44. ___

45. The *best* emergency treatment for a dog that is bleeding profusely is to
    A. apply a pressure bandage
    B. locate the source and elevate that part of the dog
    C. give aspirin to relieve the pain
    D. tie a rope below the wound
    E. keep the dog quiet and cover him with a blanket

45. ___

46. A harness is preferable to a collar
    A. during a training session
    B. with the larger breeds such as the Great Danes
    C. with miniature breeds
    D. with toy breeds
    E. with neckless dogs such as the Pugs

46. ___

47. The *best* way to hold a dog that might bite is to
    A. grasp the neck-folds, one hand on each side to control the head
    B. grab the fur on the chest with one hand and the back of the neck with the other
    C. encircle the neck with both hands
    D. hold the dog's mouth shut
    E. force the dog down and place a foot on his shoulder to immobilize him

47. ___

48. *Which* of the following statements is(are) TRUE?
      I. A mongrel dog is more trainable than a pure-bred.
     II. A mongrel dog is more resistant to disease than the pure-bred.
    III. The mongrel is more intelligent than the pure-bred.
     IV. The mongrel is more affectionate than the pure-bred.

    The CORRECT answer is:
    A. II *only* B. I,II   C. I,IV   D. I,II,III,IV
    E. None of the above

48. ___

49. An *easy* and *effective* way to deskunk a dog is to douse   49. ___
    him with
    A. alcohol   B. kerosene   C. gasoline
    D. tomato juice   E. milk

50. The *most important* aspect of punishment is   50. ___
    A. method   B. tone of voice   C. who punishes the dog
    D. surprise   E. timing

KEY (CORRECT ANSWERS)

1.	D	11.	E	21.	C	31.	D	41.	D
2.	C	12.	B	22.	C	32.	E	42.	B
3.	E	13.	A	23.	D	33.	B	43.	D
4.	A	14.	E	24.	E	34.	A	44.	B
5.	E	15.	D	25.	B	35.	C	45.	A
6.	C	16.	A	26.	C	36.	E	46.	E
7.	C	17.	E	27.	C	37.	B	47.	A
8.	D	18.	A	28.	C	38.	D	48.	E
9.	E	19.	B	29.	D	39.	E	49.	D
10.	A	20.	C	30.	B	40.	C	50.	E

EXAMINATION SECTION

DIRECTIONS: Each question or incomplete statement is followed by several suggested answers or completions. Select the one that BEST answers the question or completes the statement. *PRINT THE LETTER OF THE CORRECT ANSWER IN THE SPACE AT THE RIGHT.*

1. Clipper burns may result from all of the following EXCEPT: 1. ___
   - A. Using too fine a blade on a young dog
   - B. Using the clippers against the hair's growth
   - C. Using a blade that feels too hot to the touch
   - D. Clipping a dog that has not been shampooed
   - E. Forcing a dull blade through the coat

2. The MOST humane approach to producing litters is to mate the female   2. ___
   - A. every other heat cycle
   - B. every other year
   - C. during her first heat cycle
   - D. during each heat cycle up to the age of five years old
   - E. during the first three of every five heat cycles

3. A potbelly, lack of appetite, and diarrhea indicate the dog may have   3. ___
   - A. rabies   B. dropsy   C. worms   D. mites
   - E. impacted anal glands

4. The disease that is contracted *directly* through flies that have come from infected quarters is   4. ___
   - A. Leptospirosis   B. Distemper   C. Hepatitis
   - D. Canine Herpesvirus   E. Coccidiosis

5. People should not let their skin come into contact with a dog infected with   5. ___
   - A. ringworm   B. tapeworm   C. eczema   D. whipworm
   - E. heartworm

6. *Which* of the following statements is(are) TRUE?   6. ___
   - I. Hip Dysplasia is more common among the toy and miniature breeds, selectively bred to reduce their size.
   - II. Hip Dysplasia is hereditary.
   - III. Hip Dysplasia is more common among brood bitches.
   - IV. Hip Dysplasia is mainly seen in the older dog as part of the aging process.

   The CORRECT answer is:
   - A. I *only*   B. III,IV   C. II *only*   D. All of the above
   - E. None of the above

7. *How often* does the average female dog have a heat period?   7. ___
   - A. About every twenty-eight days
   - B. About every other month
   - C. About twice a year
   - D. Only once a year
   - E. On the average of one every eighteen months

8. On a short-term basis, liver should be fed daily if the   8. ____
   dog
   A. has loose bowels   B. has chronic diarrhea
   C. is vomiting   D. has gastritis
   E. is constipated

9. The MOST effective way to correct a dog is to   9. ____
   A. pounce on him when he least suspects it
   B. soundly strike his muzzle
   C. snap a rolled newspaper on your hand next to his ear
   D. show him your extreme displeasure
   E. threaten violence

10. All of the following are useful mineral supplements EXCEPT 10. ____
    A. potassium   B. fluorine   C. phosphorus
    D. magnesium   E. copper

11. Head shaking is symptomatic of   11. ____
    A. nervousness   B. ear trouble   C. a fit
    D. distemper   E. ringworm

12. *Which* of the following is(are) effective ways to restore 12. ____
    respiration?
      I. Slap the dog's side and swing him by his hind legs
     II. Lay the dog on his side and press firmly over the ribs
         and release
    III. Clear his mouth and give the dog's chest a sharp rap
     IV. Pinch the dog's genitals
      V. Hold the dog's mouth closed and blow into his nostrils

    The CORRECT answer is:
    A. III *only*   B. III,V   C. II,V   D. II,III,V
    E. All of the above

13. Cold compresses   13. ____
    A. only chill the animal
    C. reduce swelling   B. relieve pain
    E. help empty anal glands   D. help drain abscesses

14. If you are uncertain whether a wound is arterial or venous, 14. ____
    you *should*
    A. apply a tourniquet above the wound
    B. apply a tourniquet below the wound
    C. give artificial respiration
    D. treat for shock
    E. apply a pressure bandage

15. All of the following are good rules to follow in nursing a 15. ____
    sick dog back to health EXCEPT:
    A. Keep the dog warm
    B. Stay with him and offer reassurance
    C. Keep him clean
    D. Keep him in a dimly lit room
    E. If he is very weak, turn him regularly

2

16. The diabetic dog requires a diet that is
    A. *high* in protein, *low* in carbohydrates
    B. *high* in carbohydrates, *low* in protein
    C. *high* in carbohydrates, *low* in fats
    D. *high* in minerals, *low* in protein
    E. *high* in proteins, *low* in vitamins

16. ___

17. When taking a dog's temperature, the thermometer should remain in
    A. fifteen seconds   B. thirty seconds   C. one minute
    D. three minutes   E. four minutes

17. ___

18. The anti-bodies a puppy receives from the mother's first milk protect him
    A. for eight to ten weeks   B. for one month
    C. until the puppy is weaned D. for six months
    E. for one year

18. ___

19. A good household remedy to treat burns and scalds is
    A. bicarbonate of soda   B. cooled, strong coffee
    C. cooled, strong tea   D. whiskey
    E. olive oil

19. ___

20. All of the following are hereditary EXCEPT
    A. Hip Dysplasia   B. St. Vitus' Dance
    C. Entropion   D. Progressive Retinal Atrophy
    E. Patella Luxation

20. ___

21. An outdoor dog-house should be
    A. located where there is the most sun
    B. heated
    C. located in the shade, under trees
    D. sealed with a good-grade lead paint
    E. raised above the ground on a platform

21. ___

22. The *normal* vaginal discharge of a female following whelping is
    A. black with some mucous   B. creamy, somewhat foul-smelling
    C. light red   D. bloody with mucous
    E. greenish-brown

22. ___

23. *Which* of the following prevent(s) rickets, bone malformation, and loss of muscle tone?
    I. Calcium   II. Phosphorus   III. Niacin
    IV. Vitamin K   V. Vitamin D

    The CORRECT answer is:
    A. I *only*   B. I,III   C. I,II,V   D. I,III,V
    E. All of the above

23. ___

24. Dried skim milk is a source of supply for all of the following EXCEPT
    A. Vitamin E   B. calcium   C. phosphorous
    D. potassium   E. pantothenic acid

24. ___

25. Hemophilia is a _____ trait.   25. ____
    A. dominant   B. recessive   C. breed   D. sex-linked
    E. nutrition-linked

26. If one puppy shows a genetic defect, *what* fraction of the   26. ____
    litter will be carriers of it?
    A. One-fourth   B. One-third   C. One-half
    D. Two-thirds   E. All of them

27. Visual detection in the dog's stool or the hair around the   27. ____
    anus is possible for
    A. ringworm   B. tapeworm   C. hookworm
    D. whipworm   E. heartworm

28. All of the following are symptoms of diabetes *EXCEPT*   28. ____
    A. excessive thirst and urination
    B. excessive glucose in the blood
    C. diarrhea   D. vomiting   E. fits

29. *Which* of the following suggest the presence of worms?   29. ____
    I. A dull coat   II. Pot-bellied appearance
    III. Vomiting   IV. Diarrhea
    V. Subnormal temperature

    The CORRECT answer is:
    A. II,II   V. II,IV   C. I,II,IV
    D. I,II,III,IV   E. I,II,III,IV,V

30. The *principal* cause of disease and death in unvaccinated   30. ____
    dogs is from
    A. Hepatitis   B. Distemper   C. Canine Herpevirus
    D. Canine Tracheobronchitis   E. Leptospirosis

31. The *most common* ailment among dogs is   31. ____
    A. Hip Dysplasia   B. Arthritis   C. Worms
    D. Distemper   E. Gastroenteritis

32. Elongated Soft Palate is *more common* among   32. ____
    A. toy breeds   B. larger breeds   C. puppies
    D. short-nosed breeds
    E. breeds with long backs and short legs

33. Generally, heart problems occur *more frequently* among   33. ____
    A. the giant breeds   B. the smaller breeds
    C. males   D. females   E. castrated males

34. A loud, honking noise accompanying breathing is symptomatic   34. ____
    of
    A. Elongated Soft Palalte   B. Distemper
    C. Valvular Heart Disease   D. Kennel Cough
    E. Collapsing Trachea

35. A protozoan disease in dogs is   35. ____
    A. Coccidiosis   B. Ringworm   C. Canine Ehrlichiosis
    D. Salmonellosis   E. Hepatitis

4

36. *Which* of the following are TRUE?   36. ___
    I. A personality change is an effect on rabies.
    II. Vomiting and diarrhea are symptoms of rabies.
    III. Neurologic problems are an effect of rabies.
    IV. A rabid dog is unable to swallow water.
    V. A rabid dog is lame.

    The CORRECT answer is:
    A. III,V   B. II,IV   C. I,III,IV
    D. All of the above   E. None of the above

37. An indication that the anal glands may have to be emptied   37. ___
    is
    A. diarrhea
    B. the dog slides his rear along the floor or ground
    C. the dog chases his tail
    D. a dull coat
    E. a bloody discharge

38. The minerals needed in the *largest* quantity in the dog's   38. ___
    diet are
    A. sodium and chlorine   B. calcium and potassium
    C. calcium and phosphorous D. calcium and iron
    E. potassium and iron

39. Dogs are able to manufacture   39. ___
    A. Vitamin C   B. Vitamin A   C. Vitamin E
    D. Vitamin B_{12} E. Riboflavin, B_2

40. Of the following, *which* is(are) TRUE?   40. ___
    I. All breeds mature at the same rate.
    II. High doses of vitamins and minerals will enable the
        dog to achieve the maximum height and weight of his
        breed.
    III. All breeds have about the same life span.
    IV. All breeds have the same nutritional needs.

    The CORRECT answer is:
    A. I,II,IV   B. I,IV   C. IV *only*
    D. All of the above   E. None of the above

41. If a puppy is encouraged to eat more than he wants, he will 41. ___
    A. grow faster   B. develop better muscle tone
    C. always overeat throughout his life D. defecate more often
    E. grow larger

42. Of the following, *which* is(are) TRUE? An all-meat diet   42. ___
    I. should only be fed to puppies because they need its
       high calcium content
    II. is actually deficient in calcium
    III. interferes with the absorption of calcium
    IV. makes the dog more aggressive
    V. accustoms the dog to the taste of blood and makes him a
       better hunter

    The CORRECT answer is:
    A. I *only*   B. I,IV,V   C. II,III
    D. All of the above
    E. None of the above

43. *Which* of the following is(are) symptomatic of heat pro-
tration?
   I. Soaring temperature   II. Struggling for breath
 III. Sore, red eyes   IV. Erratic trembling

   The CORRECT answer is:
   A. I *only*   B. I,II   C. I,III   D. I,II,IV
   E. I,II,III

                                              43. ___

44. *Which* of the following is the *correct* order of the female
reproductive cycle?
   A. Festrum, metestrum, proestrum, anestrum
   B. Proestrum, estrum, metestrum, anestrum
   C. Proestrum, estrum, anestrum, metestrum
   D. Estrum, proestrum, metestrum, anestrum
   E. Anestrum, estrum, metestrum, preostrum

                                              44. ___

45. *Which* of the following conditions make a dog *unfit* for
breeding purposes?
   I. Hip Dysplasia   II. Cryptorchidism
 III. Patellar Luxation   IV. Elongated Soft Palate
   V. Progressive Retinal ATrophy

   The CORRECT answer is:
   A. I,III, IV   B. II,V   C. I,III,IV,V
   D. All of the above
   E. None of the above

                                              45. ___

46. Puppies are very sensitive to
   A. temperature   B. sound   C. odors   D. light
   E. strangers

                                              46. ___

47. Canine Brucellosis causes
   A. abortion in females   B.toxic milk in the female
   C. inability to lactate   D.birth defects
   E. cannibalism

                                            47. ___

48. *Which* of the following is(are) TRUE?
   I. Spaying prevents uterine infection.
  II. Spaying prevents false pregnancy.
 III. Spaying prevents ovarian tumors.
  IV. Spaying causes obesity.
   V. Spaying causes personality changes.

   The CORRECT answer is:
   A. I,III   B. I *only*   C. I,II,III   D. I,II,III,IV
   E. I,II,III,IV,V

                                            48. ___

49. Excessive amounts of liver in a dog's diet can cause
   A. dehydration   B. toes that splay
   C. a thiamine deficiency   D. dermatitis
   E. bone lesions

                                            49. ___

50. The *best* treatment for heat prostration is to
    A. keep the dog quiet and cover him with a light blanket
    B. give him whiskey
    C. give him black coffee with sugar
    D. flood him with cold water
    E. force him to drink cold water

50. ____

KEY (CORRECT ANSWERS)

1.	B	11.	B	21.	E	31.	C	41.	D
2.	A	12.	D	22.	E	32.	D	42.	C
3.	C	13.	C	23.	C	33.	B	43.	B
4.	E	14.	E	24.	A	34.	E	44.	C
5.	A	15.	B	25.	D	35.	A	45.	D
6.	C	16.	A	26.	D	36.	C	46.	A
7.	C	17.	C	27.	B	37.	B	47.	A
8.	E	18.	A	28.	E	38.	C	48.	C
9.	D	19.	C	29.	E	39.	A	49.	E
10.	B	20.	B	30.	B	40.	C	50.	D

EXAMINATION SECTION

DIRECTIONS: Each question or incomplete statement is followed by several suggested answers or completions. Select the one that BEST answers the question or completes the statement. *PRINT THE LETTER OF THE CORRECT ANSWER IN THE SPACE AT THE RIGHT.*

1. The condition known as "Stud Tail" is *most common* among
    A. uncastrated male cats who are confined to the home
    B. neutered male cats who are confined to the home
    C. neutered male cats kept with whole females
    D. whole male cats kept with neutered females
    E. neutered male cats who are allowed to roam outdoors

1. ___

2. Raw fish, especially freshwater fish, contains thiaminase that
    A. can prevent constipation in cats
    B. destroys the B vitamin, thiamine
    C. enables the cat to synthesize certain vitamins
    D. contributes to the development of the nervous system
    E. can cause severe skeletal problems

2. ___

3. A kitten's caloric needs are about
    A. half as much as an adult cat's requirements
    B. the same as an adult cat's requirements
    C. twice as much as an adult cat's requirements
    D. double the kitten's body weight
    E. forty calories per pound of body weight daily

3. ___

4. A virus that *primarily* attacks the mouth and lungs is
    A. Calicivirus   B. Panleukopenia   C. Pneumonitis
    D. Rhinotracheitis   E. Herpesvirus

4. ___

5. *Which* of the following can be prevented by vaccination?
    I. Calicivirus   II. Panleukopenia   III. Pneumonitis
    IV. Pansteatitis   V. Feline Infectious Peritonitis

    The CORRECT answer is:
    A. I,II   B. II,III   C. II,V   D. I,II,V
    E. All of the above

5. ___

6. *Which* of the following is relatively rare among cats?
    A. Protozoan-Coccidia   B. Hookworm   C. Tapeworm
    D. Roundworm   E. Heartworm

6. ___

7. *Which* of the following is(are) TRUE of Rhinothracheitis?   7. ____
    I. It infects only cats
   II. It is a herpesvirus
  III. It attacks the eye lining and upper breathing tubes
   IV. Infected pregnant cats may abort
    V. A vaccine is available by injection or eye drops

    The CORRECT answer is:
    A. I,III   B. II,III,IV   C. IV *only*   D. I,II,III,IV
    E. All of the above

8. *Which* of the following are TRUE?   8. ____
    I. Garlic does not cure worms
   II. Cats can transmit pinworms to children
  III. Candy does not cause worms
   IV. Worms can cause disease
    V. A ravenous appetite indicates worm infestation

    The CORRECT answer is:
    A. II,IV,V   B. I,III,IV   C. I,II,IV,V
    D. All of the above   E. None of the above

9. Most adult cats have developed an immunity to: 9. ____
    I. Ascarids   II. Tapeworm   III. Strongyloides
    IV. Protozoan-Coccidia   V. Protozoan-Toxaplasmosis

    The CORRECT answer is:
    A. II *only*   B. I,IV   C. II,IV   D. IV,V
    E. None of the above

10. *Which* of the following can infect kittens by larvae passed 10. ____
    in the mother's milk?
    I. Heartworm   II. Hookworm   III. Protozoan-Toxoplasmosis
    IV. Roundworm   V. Tapeworm

    The CORRECT answer is:
    A. II,IV   B. IV,V   C. II,IV,V   D. I,II,IV,V
    E. All of the above

11. Severe anemia, weakness, and bloody diarrhea are signs of 11. ____
    A. Protozoan-Toxoplasmosis   B. Roundworm   C. Tapeworm
    D. Hookworm   E. Heartworm

12. Protozoan-Toxoplasmosis is spread by   12. ____
    A. air transmission   B. contact with parasitic feces
    C. eating infected raw meat, rodents, or birds
    D. eating infected insects
    E. penetration through the skin

13. Highly infectious to humans is   13. ____
    A. Protozoan-Toxoplasmosis   B. Hookworm   C. Tapeworm
    D. Protozoan-Coccidia   E. Roundworm

14. Daily use of mineral oil to prevent constipation may be   14. ___
    harmful because it can cause deficiencies of all these
    fat soluble vitamins EXCEPT Vitamin
       A. A   B. E   C. K   D. B   E. D

15. *Which* of the following will induce vomiting in the cat?   15. ___
       I. Hydrogen peroxide solution
      II. Milm of magnesia
     III. Mustard and warm water solution
      IV. One-two teaspoons of salt on the back of the tongue
       V. White petroleum jelly applied to the cat's nose

    The CORRECT answer is:
       A. II *only*   B. I,II   C. II,V   D. I,III,IV
       E. II,III,V

16. A way to help prevent urinary problems in the male cat is   16. ___
    to
       A. increase the cat's intake ot milk and milk products
          such as yogurt
       B. administer female hormones
       C. feed a moist cat food with high ash content
       D. feed a dry cat food to inhibit frequent urination
       E. add salt to the diet to increase water intake and pro-
          mote urination

17. To insure that the cat swallows medication,   17. ___
       A. tap the cat's nose with a finger
       B. squeeze the folds of skin on the side of the neck
       C. stroke the cat's neck
       D. rub the cat's stomach
       E. place a thumb on one side and fingers on the other,
          and press hard against and under the upper teeth

18. The BEST treatment for a frostbitten ear or tail is to   18. ___
       A. apply a pressure bandage to the affected area
       B. cover the affected area with warm, moist towels
       C. cover the affected area with dry, hot towels
       D. rub the affected area
       E. gently squeeze the affected area

19. *Which* of the following are *good* urinary acidifiers?   19. ___
       I. Vitamin C   II. Magnesium   III. Yogurt
      IV. Tomato juice   V. Cranberry juice

    The CORRECT answer is:
       A. I,III,V   B. II,III   C. I,IV,V   D. I,II,IV,V
       E. II,IV,V

20. All of the following are signs of third degree burns EXCEPT 20. ___
    the.
       A. skin is black   B. skin is pearly white
       C. skin is red   D. hair falls out
       E. burn is painless

3

21. Alkali burns can be neutralized by applying   21. ____
       A. sodium bicarbonate   B. dishwater granules
       C. olive oil   D. egg whites   E. vinegar

22. Begin emergency treatment for heatstroke if the cat's tem-   22. ____
    perature reaches
       A. 98.6°   B. 100°   C. 101.5°   D. 103°   E. 105°

23. Paper Bone Disease (Osteoporosis) may be prevented by   23. ____
       A. vaccination   B. proper exercise
       C. reducing caloric intake
       D. providing adequate amounts of calcium and phosphorus
       E. providing adequate amounts of thiamine

24. Rodent Ulcer manifests itself   24. ____
       A. on the upper lip   B. in the armpits
       C. on the ear flaps   D. on the chin
       E. on the base of the tail

25. The *major* signs of shock are: 25. ____
         I. Pale or muddy gums   II. Uneven pupil size
       III. Weak and rapid pulse   IV. Rapid breathing
         V. Low rectal temperature

    The CORRECT answer is:
       A. I,II,V   B. III,IV   C. I,II,III,V
       D. I,III,IV,V   E. All of the above

26. *Which* of the following skin problems of the cat is in-   26. ____
    fectious to humans?
       A. Allergic Inhalent Dermatitis   B. Rodent Ulcer
       C. Contact Dermatitis   D. Feline Acne
       E. Ringworm

27. Pseudocoprostasis is *most common* among   27. ____
       A. kittens   B. outdoor cats   C. castrated males
       D. long-haired cats   E. short-nosed cats

28. *Which* of the following is(are) TRUE of Cystitis?   28. ____
         I. It is more common among male cats
        II. The cat urinates more frequently with the condition
       III. A normally housebroken cat will urinate outside the
            litter box
        IV. The male cat will frequently lick his penis
         V. There is blood in the urine

    The CORRECT answer is:
       A. II,III   V. IV *only*   C. I *only*   D. II,III,IV,V
       E. All of the above

29. *Which* of the following are "female" ailments?   29. ____
         I. Pyometra   II. Cystitis   III. Mastitis
        IV. Pseudocoprostasis   V. Eclampsia

    The CORRECT answer is:
       A. I,V   B. II,III,IV   C. I,III,V   D. II,III,V
       E. All of the above

4

30. A highly contagious virus that *primarily* attacks the bone   30. ___
    marrow and intestines is
    A. Calicivirus   B. Panleukopenia   C. Rhineotracheitis
    D. Rabies   E. Pneumonitis

31. *Which* of the following breeds are closely related to the   31. ___
    Siamese?
    I. Burmese   II. Exotic Short Hair   III. Abyssinian
    IV. British Short Hair   V. Colorpoint Short Hair

    The CORRECT answer is:
    A. II,III   B. I,IV,V   C. I,III
    D. All of the above   E. None of the above

32. The Himalayan breed was developed from the   32. ___
    A. Oriental Short Hair - Korat hybrids
    B. Exotic Short Hair - Balinese hybrids
    C. Siamese - Persian hybrids
    D. Turkish Angora - Abyssinian hybrids
    E. Colorpoint Short Hair - Egyptian Mau hybrids

33. A tip or touch of one color at the end of a hair of another   33. ___
    color is called
    A. ticking   **B. tipping**   C. points
    D. **classic tabby**   E. bi-color

34. The Sacred Cat of Burma with a characteristic creamy, gold   34. ___
    longhair coat ,with brown or blue points and white paws ,
    describes the
    A. Birman   B. Himalayan   C. Burmese
    D. Balinese E. Korat

35. *Which* of the following is an *accurate* description of the   35. ___
    Korat?   A
    A. long-haired Siamese
    B. cat with only an undercoat of extremely soft and silky
       hair, free of coarse or guard hairs
    C. cat with a long, fine angular line of a Siamese but with
       conventional color patterns
    D. cat with a unique set to its eyes, high cheekbones, and
       a short tail fanned out like a pom-pom
    E. solid blue cat with a heavy, silvery sheen and huge
       prominent green or amber-green eyes

36. A breed that is a cross between the Siamese and Burmese is   36. ___
    the
    A. Birman   B. Somali   C. Tonkinese
    D. Exotic Short Hair   E. Oriental Short Hair

37. The darker coloration, sometimes seen on the face, paws,   37. ___
    ears, and tails of certain breeds is called the
    A. ticks   B. points   C. tips   D. laces   E. lockets

5

38. "Belling the Cat" is an expression used to describe having it   38. _
    A. mated   B. neutered   C. tattooed   D. declawed   E. weaned

39. The process of birth in cats is called   39. _
    I. whelping   II. quickening   III. kittening
    IV. queening   V. catting

    The CORRECT answer is:
    A. II *only*   B. III,V   C. III,IV   D. II,III,IV,V
    E. All of the above

40. A "Queen" is a   40. _
    A. neutered male cat   B. female cat
    C. pregnant cat   D. kitten of either sex
    E. show cat of either sex

41. For *which* of the following should a cat be vaccinated?   41. _
    I. Rabies   II. Leptospirosis   III. Panleukopenia
    IV. Respiratory infections   V. Coccidiosis

    The CORRECT answer is:
    A. I,IV   B. I *only*   C. II,III,IV   D. I,III,IV
    E. All of the above

42. An adult cat has _____ teeth.   42. _
    A. thirty   B. thirty-two   C. thirty-six   D. forty
    E. forty-two

43. *Which* of the following should be avoided in the cat's diet?   43. _
    A. Raw vegetables   B. Raw fish   C. Uncooked egg yolks
    D. Lukewarm milk   E. Cheese

44. An acute or chronic inflammation of the urinary bladder of   44. _
    cats is
    A. pyometra   B. coccidiosis   C. cryptococcosis
    D. cystitis   E. nephritis

45. *Which* of the following should be recognized as symptoms of   45. _
    conjunctivitis?
    I. Excessive tearing
    II. Movement of the third eyelid to partially obscure the eye
    III. A sticky, opaque white or yellow discharge from one or both
        nostrils
    IV. A sticky, yellowish discharge which accumulates at the medial
        corners of the eye
    V. A persistent cough and weight loss

    The CORRECT answer is:
    A. I,II.III   B. I,II,IV   C. III,V   D. I,IV
    E. I,III,IV,V

46. Common among older cats is decreased kidney function due to   46. _
    aging. If this occurs,
    A. substitute milk for water
    B. allow the cat to drink as much water as it wants
    C. restrict water consumption
    D. permit no water in the evening
    E. feed only a dry cat-food diet

6

47. Female cats ovulate
    A. once a month   B. twice a year
    C. in response to changing hours of daylight
    D. in response to changing temperature
    E. in response to breeding

47. ___

48. Pansteatitis results from a deficiency of
    A. Vitamin E   B. Vitamin A   C. Vitamin K
    D. Thiamine   E. Vitamin D

48. ___

49. The BEST way to restrain a cat is to
    A. put it on a leash   B. place a walking harness on it
    C. wrap it in a blanket   D. tie a cloth bag over its head
    E. tape its mouth closed

49. ___

50. Of the following poisons and remedies, *which* are CORRECTLY
    matched?
      I. Bleach - induce vomiting
     II. Weed killer - induce vomiting
    III. Gasoline - do   not induce vomiting
     IV. Paint thinner or remover - do   not induce vomiting
      V. Acetone - do   not induce vomiting

    The CORRECT answer is:
    A. III,IV,V   B. I,II,IV   C. II,III,IV,V   D. I,II,III,IV
    E. All of the above

50. ___

KEY (CORRECT ANSWERS)

1.	A	11.	D	21.	E	31.	B	41.	D
2.	B	12.	C	22.	E	32.	C	42.	A
3.	C	13.	A	23.	D	33.	A	43.	B
4.	A	14.	D	24.	A	34.	A	44.	D
5.	A	15.	D	25.	D	35.	E	45.	D
6.	E	16.	E	26.	E	36.	C	46.	B
7.	E	17.	A	27.	D	37.	B	47.	E
8.	B	18.	B	28.	E	38.	D	48.	A
9.	B	19.	C	29.	C	39.	B	49.	C
10.	A	20.	C	30.	B	40.	B	50.	D

EXAMINATION SECTION
TEST 1

Directions: Each question or incomplete statement is followed by several suggested answers or completions. Select the one that BEST answers the question or completes the statement. *PRINT THE LETTER OF THE CORRECT ANSWER IN THE SPACE AT THE RIGHT.*

1) When conducting a needs assessment for the purpose of education planning, an agency's FIRST step is to identify or provide

1._____

   A. a profile of population characteristics
   B. barriers to participation
   C. existing resources
   D. profiles of competing resources

2) Research has demonstrated that of the following, the most effective medium for communicating with external publics is/are

2._____

   A. video news releases
   B. television
   C. radio
   D. newspapers

3) Basic ideas behind the effort to influence the attitudes and behaviors of a constituency include each of the following, EXCEPT the idea that

3._____

   A. words, rather than actions or events, are most likely to motivate
   B. demands for action are a usual response
   C. self-interest usually figures heavily into public involvement
   D. the reliability of change programs is difficult to assess

4) An agency representative is trying to craft a pithy message to constituents in order to encourage the use agency program resources. Choosing an audience for such messages is easiest when the message

4._____

   A. is project- or behavior-based
   B. is combined with other messages
   C. is abstract
   D. has a broad appeal

5) Of the following factors, the most important to the success of an
agency's external education or communication programs is the

5._____

A. amount of resources used to implement them
B. public's prior experiences with the agency
C. real value of the program to the public
D. commitment of the internal audience

6) A representative for a state agency is being interviewed by a reporter
from a local news network. The representative is being asked to defend a program that is extremely unpopular in certain parts of the municipality. When a
constituency is known to be opposed to a position, the most useful communication strategy is to present

6._____

A. only the arguments that are consistent with constituents' views
B. only the agency's side of the issue
C. both sides of the argument as clearly as possible
D. both sides of the argument, omitting key information about the oppos-
ing position

7) The most significant barriers to effective agency community relations
include

7._____

I. widespread distrust of communication strategies
II. the media's "watchdog" stance
III. public apathy
IV. statutory opposition

A. I only
B. I and II
C. II and III
D. III and IV

8) In conducting an education program, many agencies use workshops
and seminars in a classroom setting. Advantages of classroom-style teach-
ing over other means of educating the public include each of the following,
EXCEPT:

8._____

A. enabling an instructor to verify learning through testing and interaction
with the target audience
B. enabling hands-on practice and other participatory learning techniques
C. ability to reach an unlimited number of participants in a given length
of time
D. ability to convey the latest, most up-to-date information

9) The _____ model of community relations is character-
ized by an attempt to persuade the public to adopt the agency's point of view.

9. _____

A. two-way symmetric
B. two-way asymmetric
C. public information
D. press agency/publicity

10) Important elements of an internal situation analysis include the

10. _____

    I. list of agency opponents
    II. communication audit
    III. updated organizational almanac
    IV. stakeholder analysis

A. I and II
B. I, II and III
C. II and III
D. I, II, III and IV

11) Government agency information efforts typically involve each of the
following objectives, EXCEPT to

11. _____

A. implement changes in the policies of government agencies to align
with public opinion
B. communicate the work of agencies
C. explain agency techniques in a way that invites input from citizens
D. provide citizen feedback to government administrators

12) Factors that are likely to influence the effectiveness of an educational
campaign include the

12. _____

    I. level of homogeneity among intended participants
    II. number and types of media used
    III. receptivity of the intended participants
    IV. level of specificity in the message or behavior to be taught

A. I and II
B. I, II and III
C. II and III
D. I, II, III and IV

13)   An agency representative is writing instructional objectives that will   13. _____
later help to measure the effectiveness of an educational program. Which of
the following verbs, included in an objective, would be MOST helpful for the
purpose of measuring effectiveness?

A.   Know
B.   Identify
C.   Learn
D.   Comprehend

14)   A state education agency wants to encourage participation in a pro-   14. _____
gram that has just received a boost through new federal legislation. The program is intended to include participants from a wide variety of socioeconomic
and other demographic characteristics.
       The agency wants to launch a broad-based program that will inform
virtually every interested party in the state about the program's new circumstances. In attempting to deliver this message to such a wide-ranging constituency, the agency's best practice would be to

A.   broadcast the same message through as many different media channels
as possible
B.   focus on one discrete segment of the public at a time
C.   craft a message whose appeal is as broad as the public itself
D.   let the program's achievements speak for themselves and rely on word-
of-mouth

15)   Advantages associated with using the World Wide Web as an educa-   15. _____
tional tool include

       I.   an appeal to younger generations of the public
       II.   visually-oriented, interactive learning
       III. learning that is not confined by space, time, or institutional as
             sociation
       IV.   a variety of methods for verifying use and learning

A.   I only
B.   I and II
C.   I, II and III
D.   I, II, III and IV

16) In agencies involved in health care, community relations is a critical function because it

16._____

A. serves as an intermediary between the agency and consumers
B. generates a clear mission statement for agency goals and priorities
C. ensures patient privacy while satisfying the media's right to information
D. helps marketing professionals determine the wants and needs of agency constituents

17) After an extensive campaign to promote its newest program to constituents, an agency learns that most of the audience did not understand the intended message. Most likely, the agency has

17._____

A. chosen words that were intended to inform, rather than persuade
B. not accurately interpreted what the audience really needed to know
C. overestimated the ability of the audience to receive and process the message
D. compensated for noise that may have interrupted the message

18) The necessary elements that lead to conviction and motivation in the minds of participants in an educational or information program include each of the following, EXCEPT the _____ of the message.

18._____

A. acceptability
B. intensity
C. single-channel appeal
D. pervasiveness

19) Printed materials are often at the core of educational programs provided by public agencies. The primary disadvantage associated with print is that it

19._____

A. does not enable comprehensive treatment of a topic
B. is generally unreliable in term of assessing results
C. is often the most expensive medium available
D. is constrained by time

20) Traditional thinking on public opinion holds that there is about _____ _____ percent of the public who are pivotal to shifting the balance and momentum of opinion—they are concerned about an issue, but not fanatical, and interested enough to pay attention to a reasoned discussion.

20._____

A. 2
B. 10
C. 33
D. 51

21) One of the most useful guidelines ...change among people ...lel of community relations... is to ...lic to adopt the agency's ...   21. _____

A. inviting ... the target audience to ...proaching them
B. use mo... ral appeals as the primary
C. use con... crete images to enable p...behaviors or indifference
D. offer ta... ngible rewards to people
...al situation analysis inclu...

22) An age... ncy is attempting to eval... educational   22. _____
program. For ... this purpose, it wants to ...ps discussing the same p... rogram. Which of the fol...uideline for
the use of focu... ...almanac ... s groups?

A. Focus ... groups should only inclu...ated in the program.
B. Be sure ... to accurately record the ...
C. The sa... ne questions should be a...meeting.
D. It is oft... en helpful to have a neut... facilitate discussions.
...n efforts typically involve

23) Resear... ch consistently shows tha... determinant   23. _____
most likely to ... make a newspaper editor
...ies of government agencie...

A. novelty ...cies
B. promin... way that invites input fro... ence
C. proxim... ...ernment administrators ...ity
D. conflic... t

...ice the effectiveness of an
24) Which ... of the following is NOT ... to take into   24. _____
account when ... considering a population ...

A. State o... ...nong intended participant... f program development
...dia used
B. Resour... ed participants ces available
C. Demog... ... message or behavior to ... ...raphics
D. Comm... unity attitudes

25) The fir... st step in any communica...   25. _____

A. develo... p a research instrument
B. determ... ine how the organization ...
C. hire a c... ontractor
D. determ... ine which audience to ass...

KEY (CORRECT ANSWERS)

1. A
2. D
3. A
4. A
5. D

6. C
7. D
8. C
9. B
10. C

11. A
12. D
13. B
14. B
15. C

16. A
17. B
18. C
19. B
20. B

21. C
22. A
23. C
24. C
25. D

TEST 2

Directions: Each question or incomplete statement is followed by several suggested answers or completions. Select the one that BEST answers the question or completes the statement. *PRINT THE LETTER OF THE CORRECT ANSWER IN THE SPACE AT THE RIGHT.*

1)   A public relations practitioner at an agency has just composed a press release highlighting a program's recent accomplishments and success stories. In pitching such releases to print outlets, the practitioner should

      I.   e-mail, mail, or send them by messenger
      II.   address them to "editor" or "news director"
      III.   have an assistant call all media contacts by telephone
      IV.   ask reporters or editors how they prefer to receive them

A.   I and II
B.   I and IV
C.   II, III and IV
D.   III only

2)   The "output goals" of an educational program are MOST likely to include

A.   specified ratings of services by participants on a standardized scale
B.   observable effects on a given community or clientele
C.   the number of instructional hours provided
D.   the number of participants served

3)   An agency wants to evaluate satisfaction levels among program participants, and mails out questionnaires to everyone who has been enrolled in the last year. The primary problem associated with this method of evaluative research is that it

A.   poses a significant inconvenience for respondents
B.   is inordinately expensive
C.   does not allow for follow-up or clarification questions
D.   usually involves a low response rate

4)   A communications audit is an important tool for measuring

A.   the depth of penetration of a particular message or program
B.   the cost of the organization's information campaigns
C.   how key audiences perceive an organization
D.   the commitment of internal stakeholders

1. _____

2. _____

3. _____

4. _____

5) The "ABC's" of written learning objectives include each of the follow-   5. _____
ing, EXCEPT

A.   Audience
B.   Behavior
C.   Conditions
D.   Delineation

6) When attempting to change the behaviors of constituents, it is impor-   6. _____
tant to keep in mind that

I.   most people are skeptical of communications that try to get
     them to change their behaviors
II. in most cases, a person selects the media to which he exposes
     himself
III. people tend to react defensively to messages or programs that
     rely on fear as a motivating factor
IV. programs should aim for the broadest appeal possible in order
     to include as many participants as possible

A.   I and II
B.   I, II and III
C.   II and III
D.   I, II, III and IV

7) The "laws" of public opinion include the idea that it is   7. _____

A.   useful for anticipating emergencies
B.   not sensitive to important events
C.   basically determined by self-interest
D.   sustainable through persistent appeals

8) Which of the following types of evaluations is used to measure public   8. _____
attitudes before and after an information/educational program?

A.   retrieval study
B.   copy test
C.   quota sampling
D.   benchmark study

9) The primary source for internal communications is/are usually   9. _____

A.   flow charts
B.   meetings
C.   voice mail
D.   printed publications

10)   An agency representative is putting together informational materials—   10. _____
brochures and a newsletter—outlining changes in one of the state's biggest
benefits programs. In assembling print materials as a medium for delivering
information to the public, the representative should keep in mind each of the
following trends:

    I.   For various reasons, the reading capabilities of the public are in
        general decline
    II.   Without tables and graphs to help illustrate the changes, it is
        unlikely that the message will be delivered effectively
    III.   Professionals and career-oriented people are highly receptive to
        information written in the form of a journal article or empirical
        study
    IV.   People tend to be put off by print materials that use itemized
        and bulleted (•) lists.

A.   I and II
B.   I, II and III
C.   II and III
D.   I, II, III and IV

11)   Which of the following steps in a problem-oriented information cam-   11. _____
paign would typically be implemented FIRST?

A.   Deciding on tactics
B.   Determining a communications strategy
C.   Evaluating the problem's impact
D.   Developing an organizational strategy

12)   A common pitfall in conducting an educational program is to   12. _____

A.   aim it at the wrong target audience
B.   overfund it
C.   leave it in the hands of people who are in the business of education,
rather than those with expertise in the business of the organization
D.   ignore the possibility that some other organization is meeting the same
educational need for the target audience

13)   The key factors that affect the credibility of an agency's educational   13. _____
program include

A.   organization
B.   scope
C.   sophistication
D.   penetration

14) Research on public opinion consistently demonstrates that it is   14. _____

A.   easy to move people toward a strong opinion on anything, as long as they are approached directly through their emotions
B.   easier to move people away from an opinion they currently hold than to have them form an opinion about something they have not previously cared about
C.   easy to move people toward a strong opinion on anything, as long as the message appeals to their reason and intellect
D.   difficult to move people toward a strong opinion on anything, no matter what the approach

15) In conducting an education program, many agencies use meetings and   15. _____
conferences to educate an audience about the organization and its programs. Advantages associated with this approach include

    I.   a captive audience that is known to be interested in the topic
    II.   ample opportunities for verifying learning
    III.   cost-efficient meeting space
    IV.   the ability to provide information on a wider variety of subjects

A.   I and II
B.   I, III and IV
C.   II and III
D.   I, II, III and IV

16) An agency is attempting to evaluate the effectiveness of its educational   16. _____
programs. For this purpose, it wants to observe several focus groups discussing particular programs. For this purpose, a focus group should never number more than _____ participants.

A.   5
B.   10
C.   15
D.   20

17) A _____ speech is written so that several agency members   17. _____
can deliver it to different audiences with only minor variations.

A.   basic
B.   printed
C.   quota
D.   pattern

18)   Which of the following statements about public opinion is generally   18. _____
considered to be FALSE?

A.   Opinion is primarily reactive rather than proactive.
B.   People have more opinions about goals than about the means by which
to achieve them.
C.   Facts tend to shift opinion in the accepted direction when opinion is
not solidly structured.
D.   Public opinion is based more on information than desire.

19)   An agency is trying to promote its educational program. As a general   19. _____
rule, the agency should NOT assume that

A.   people will only participate if they perceive an individual benefit
B.   promotions need to be aimed at small, discrete groups
C.   if the program is good, the audience will find out about it
D.   a variety of methods, including advertising, special events, and direct
mail, should be considered

20)   In planning a successful educational program, probably the first and   20. _____
most important question for an agency to ask is:

A.   What will be the content of the program?
B.   Who will be served by the program?
C.   When is the best time to schedule the program?
D.   Why is the program necessary?

21)   Media kits are LEAST likely to contain   21. _____

A.   fact sheets
B.   memoranda
C.   photographs with captions
D.   news releases

22)   The use of pamphlets and booklets as media for communication with   22. _____
the public often involves the disadvantage that

A.   the messages contained within them are frequently nonspecific
B.   it is difficult to measure their effectiveness in delivering the message
C.   there are few opportunities for people to refer to them
D.   color reproduction is poor

23)   The most important prerequisite of a good educational program is an   23. _____

A.   abundance of resources to implement it
B.   individual staff unit formed for the purpose of program delivery
C.   accurate needs assessment
D.   uneducated constituency

24)   After an education program has been delivered, an agency conducts a   24. _____
program evaluation to determine whether its objectives have been met. General rules about how to conduct such an education program evaluation include
each of the following, EXCEPT that it

A.   must be done immediately after the program has been implemented
B.   should be simple and easy to use
C.   should be designed so that tabulation of responses can take place
quickly and inexpensively
D.   should solicit mostly subjective, open-ended responses if the audience
was large

25)   Using electronic media such as television as means of educating the   25. _____
public is typically recommended ONLY for agencies that

    I.   have a fairly simple message to begin with
    II.   want to reach the masses, rather than a targeted audience
    III.   have substantial financial resources
    IV.   accept that they will not be able to measure the results of the
           campaign with much precision

A.   I and II
B.   I, II and III
C.   II and IV
D.   I, II, III and IV

KEY (CORRECT ANSWERS)

1. B
2. C
3. D
4. C
5. D

6. B
7. C
8. D
9. D
10. A

11. C
12. D
13. A
14. D
15. B

16. B
17. D
18. D
19. C
20. D

21. B
22. B
23. C
24. D
25. D

EXAMINATION SECTION
TEST 1

DIRECTIONS: Each question or incomplete statement is followed by several suggested answers or completions. Select the one that BEST answers the question or completes the statement. *PRINT THE LETTER OF THE CORRECT ANSWER IN THE SPACE AT THE RIGHT.*

1. If you can't come to work in the morning because you do not feel well, you should   1.____

    A. call your supervisor and let him know that you are sick
    B. try to get someone else to take your place
    C. have your doctor call your office as proof that you are sick
    D. come to work anyway so that you won't lose your job

2. Many machines have certain safety devices for the operators.   2.____
The MOST important reason for having these safety devices is to

    A. increase the amount of work that the machines can do
    B. permit repairs to be made on the machines without shutting them down
    C. help prevent accidents to people who use the machines
    D. reduce the cost of electric power needed to run the machines

3. While working on the job, you accidentally break a window pane. No one is around, and   3.____
you are able to clean up the broken pieces of glass.
It would then be BEST for you to

    A. leave a note near the window that a new glass has to be put in because it was accidentally broken
    B. forget about the whole thing because the window was not broken on purpose
    C. write a report to your supervisor telling him that you saw a broken window pane that has to be fixed
    D. tell your supervisor that you accidentally broke the window pane while working

4. There is a two-light fixture in the room where you are working. One of the light bulbs goes   4.____
out , and you need more light to work by.
You should

    A. change the fuse in the fuse box
    B. have a new bulb put in
    C. call for an electrician and stop work until he comes
    D. find out what is causing the short circuit

5. The BEST way to remove some small pieces of broken glass from a floor is to   5.____

    A. use a brush and dust pan
    B. pick up the pieces carefully with your hands
    C. use a wet mop and a wringer
    D. sweep the pieces into the corner of the room

6. When you are not sure about some instructions that your supervisor has given you on how to do a certain job, it would be BEST for you to   6.___

    A. start doing the work and stop when you come to the part that you do not understand
    B. ask the supervisor to go over the instructions which are not clear to you
    C. do the job immediately from beginning to the end, leaving out the part that you are not sure of
    D. wait until the supervisor leaves and then ask a more experienced worker to explain the job to you

7. When an employee first comes on the job, he is given a period of training by his supervisor.   7.___
The MAIN reason for this training period is to

    A. make sure that the employee will learn to do his work correctly and safely
    B. give the employee a chance to show the supervisor that he can learn quickly
    C. allow the supervisor and the employee a chance to become friendly with each other
    D. find out which employees will make good supervisors later on

8. After you open a sealed box of supplies, you find that the box is not full and that some of the supplies are missing.   8.___
You should

    A. use fewer supplies than you intended to
    B. seal the box and take it back to the storeroom
    C. get signed statements from other employees that when you opened the box, it was not full
    D. tell your supervisor about it

9. Suppose that after you have been on the job a few months, your supervisor shows you some small mistakes you are making in your work.   9.___
You should

    A. tell your supervisor that these mistakes don't keep you from finishing your work
    B. ask your supervisor how you can avoid these mistakes
    C. try to show your supervisor that your way of doing the work is just as good as his way of doing it
    D. check with the other workers to find out if your supervisor is also finding fault with them

10. If your supervisor gives you an order to do a special job which you do not like to do, you should   10.___

    A. take a long time to do the job so that you won't get this job again
    B. do the job the best way you know how even though you don't like it
    C. make believe that you didn't hear your supervisor and do your regular work
    D. say nothing but tell another employee that the supervisor wants him to do this special job

11. If two employees who are working together on a job do not agree on how to do the job, it would be BEST   11.____

    A. for each worker to do the job in his own way until it is finished
    B. to put off doing the job until both workers agree to do it the same way
    C. to ask the supervisor to decide on the way the job is to be done
    D. for each worker to ask for a transfer to another assignment because they can't get along with each other

12. Suppose that in order to finish your work, you have to lift a heavy box off the floor onto an empty desk.   12.____
You should

    A. leave the box where it is and tell your supervisor that you have finished your work
    B. lift the box by yourself very quickly so that your supervisor will see that you are a strong, willing worker
    C. ask another employee to give you a hand to lift the box off the floor
    D. complain to your supervisor that he should check a job before giving you such a tough assignment

13. Bulletin boards for the posting of official notices are usually put up near the place where employees check in and out each day.   13.____
For an employee to spend a few minutes each day to read the new notices is

    A. *good;* these notices give him information about the Department and his own work
    B. *bad;* all important information is given to employees by their supervisors
    C. *good;* this is a way to "take a break" during the day
    D. *bad;* the notices can't help him in his work

14. Suppose that your supervisor gives you a job to do and tells you that he wants you to finish it in three hours.   14.____
If you finish the work at the end of 2 hours, you should

    A. wait until the three hours are up and then tell your supervisor that you are finished
    B. go to your supervisor and tell him that you finished a half-hour ahead of time
    C. spend the next half-hour getting ready for the next job you think your supervisor may give you
    D. take a half-hour rest period because good work deserves a reward

15. Which one of the following is it LEAST important to include in an accident report?   15.____

    A. Name and address of the injured person
    B. Date, time, and place where the accident happened
    C. Name and address of the injured person's family doctor
    D. An explanation of how the accident happened

16. If, near the end of the day, you realize that you made a mistake in your work and you can't do the work over, you should   16.____

    A. forget about it because there is only a small chance that the mistake can be traced back to you
    B. wait a few days and take the blame for the mistake if it is caught
    C. ask the other employees to keep the mistake a secret so that no one can be blamed
    D. tell your supervisor about the mistake right away

17. Employees should wipe up water spilled on floors immediately. 17.___
The BEST reason for this is that water on a floor

    A. is a sign that employees are sloppy
    B. makes for a slippery condition that could cause an accident
    C. will eat into the wax protecting the floor
    D. is against health regulations

18. Another worker, who is a good friend of yours, leaves work an hour before quitting time to 18.___
take care of a personal matter. When you leave later, you find that your friend did not sign
out on the timesheet.
For you to sign out for your friend would be

    A. *good,* because he will do the same for you some day when you want to leave early
    B. *bad,* because other employees will also want you to do the same favor for them on
       other days
    C. *good,* because the timesheet should not have any empty spaces on it
    D. *bad,* because timesheets are official records which employees should keep hon-
       estly and accurately

19. While you are working, a person asks you how to get to an office which you know is one 19.___
floor above you in the building where you work.
It would be BEST for you to tell this person that

    A. you can't answer any questions because you have to finish your work
    B. he should go back to the lobby and check the list of offices
    C. the office he is looking for is on the next floor
    D. he should call the office he is looking for to get exact instructions on how to get
       there

20. While you are at work, you find a sealed brown envelope under a desk. The envelope is 20.___
marked *Personal - Hand Delivery* and is addressed to an official who has an office in the
building where you are working.
You should

    A. drop the envelope into the nearest mailbox so that it can be delivered the next day
    B. look up the telephone number of the official and call him up to tell him what you
       have found
    C. put the envelope in your pocket and come in early the next day to deliver it person-
       ally to the official
    D. give the envelope to your supervisor right away and tell him where you found it

21. A messenger delivered 32 letters on Monday, 47 on Tuesday, 29 on Wednesday, 36 on 21.___
Thursday, and 41 on Friday.
How many letters did he deliver altogether?

    A. 157   B. 185   C. 218   D. 229

22. Mr. White paid 4% sales tax on a $95 television set. 22.___
The amount of sales tax that he paid was

    A. $9.50   B. $4.00   C. $3.80   D. $.95

23. How many square feet are there in a room which is 25 feet long and 35 feet wide?   23.____
    _____ square feet.

    A. 600   B. 750   C. 875   D. 925

24. How much would it cost to send a 34 pound package by parcel post if the postage is   24.____
    $1.60 for the first 20 pounds and 7 for each additional pound?

    A. $2.34   B. $2.58   C. $2.66   D. $2.80

25. Adding together 1/2, 3/4, and 1/8, the total is   25.____

    A. 1 1/4   B. 1 1/2   C. 1 3/8   D. 1 3/4

26. If a piece of wood 40 inches long is cut into two pieces so that the larger piece is three   26.____
    times as long as the, smaller piece, the smaller piece is _____ inches.

    A. 4   B. 5   C. 8   D. 10

27. Two friends, Smith and Jones, together spend $1,800 to buy a car.   27.____
    If Smith put up twice as much money as Jones, then Jones' share of the cost of the car
    was

    A. $300   B. $600   C. $900   D. $1,200

28. In a certain agency, two-thirds of the employees are clerks and the remainder are typists.   28.____
    If there are 180 clerks, then the number of typists in this agency is

    A. 270   B. 90   C. 240   D. 60

Questions 29-35.

DIRECTIONS: Answer Questions 29 through 35 ONLY according to the information given in
               the chart below.

EMPLOYEE RECORD

Name of Employee	Where Assigned	Number of Days Absent Vacation	Sick Leave	Yearly Salary
Carey	Laundry	18	4	$18,650
Hayes	Mortuary	24	8	$17,930
Irwin	Buildings	20	17	$18,290
King	Supply	12	10	$17,930
Lane	Mortuary	17	8	$17,750
Martin	Buildings	13	12	$17,750
Prince	Buildings	5	7	$17,750
Quinn	Supply	19	0	$17,250
Sands	Buildings	23	10	$18,470
Victor	Laundry	21	2	$18,150

29. The *only* employee who was NOT absent because of sickness is — 29.__

    A. Hayes   B. Lane   C. Victor   D. Quinn

30. The employee with the HIGHEST salary is — 30.__

    A. Carey   B. Irwin   C. Sands   D. Victor

31. The employee with the LOWEST salary is assigned to the _____ Bureau. — 31.__

    A. Laundry   B. Mortuary   C. Building   D. Supply

32. Which one of these was absent or on vacation more than 20 days? — 32.__

    A. Irwin   B. Lane   C. Quinn   D. Victor

33. The number of employees whose salary is LESS than $18,100 a year is — 33.__

    A. 4   B. 5   C. 6   D. 7

34. MOST employees are assigned to — 34.__

    A. Laundry   B. Mortuary   C. Buildings   D. Supply

35. From the chart, you can figure out for each employee — 35.__

    A. how long he has worked in his present assignment
    B. how many days vacation he has left
    C. how many times he has been late
    D. how much he earns a month

KEY (CORRECT ANSWERS)

1. A		16. D	
2. C		17. B	
3. D		18. D	
4. B		19. C	
5. A		20. D	
6. B		21. B	
7. A		22. C	
8. D		23. C	
9. B		24. B	
10. B		25. C	
11. C		26. D	
12. C		27. B	
13. A		28. B	
14. B		29. D	
15. C		30. A	

31.	D
32.	D
33.	C
34.	C
35.	D

TEST 2

Questions 1-5.

DIRECTIONS: Answer Questions 1 to 5 ONLY according to the information given in the following passage.

EMPLOYEE LEAVE REGULATIONS

Peter Smith, as a full-time permanent City employee under the Career and Salary Plan, earns an "annual leave allowance" This consists of a certain number of days off a year with pay and may be used for vacation, personal business, and for observing religious holidays. As a newly appointed employee, during his first eight years of City service, he will earn an "annual leave allowance" of twenty days off a year (an average of 1 2/3 days off a month). After he has finished eight full years of working for the City, he will begin earning an additional five days off a year. His "annual leave allowance," therefore, will then be twenty-five days a year and will remain at this amount for seven full years. He will begin earning an additional two days off a year after he has completed a total of fifteen years of City employment. Therefore, in his sixteenth year of working for the City, Mr. Smith will be earning twenty-seven days off a year as his "annual leave allowance" (an average of 2 1/4 days off a month).

A "sick leave allowance" of one day a month is also given to Mr. Smith, but it can be used only in case of actual illness. When Mr. Smith returns to work after using "sick leave allowance," he must have a doctor's note if the absence is for a total of more than three days, but he may also be required to show a doctor's note for absences of one, two, or three days.

1. According to the above passage, Mr. Smith's *annual leave allowance* consists of a certain number of days off a year which he

    A.   does not get paid for
    B.   gets paid for at time and a half
    C.   may use for personal business
    D.   may not use for observing religious holidays

1._____

2. According to the above passage, after Mr. Smith has been working for the City for nine years, his *annual leave allowance* will be _____ days a year.

    A. 20   B. 25   C. 27   D. 37

2._____

3. According to the above passage, Mr. Smith will begin earning an average of 2 1/4 days off a month as his *annual leave allowance* after he has worked for the City for _____ full years.

    A. 7   B. 8   C. 15   D. 17

3._____

4. According to the above passage, Mr. Smith is given a *sick leave allowance* of

    A.   1 day every 2 months   B.   1 day per month
    C.   1 2/3 days per month   D.   2 1/4 days a month

4._____

5. According to the above passage, when he uses *sick leave allowance,* Mr. Smith may be required to show a doctor's note   5.___

    A. even if his absence is for only 1 day
    B. only if his absence is for more than 2 days
    C. only if his absence is for more than 3 days
    D. only if his absence is for 3 days or more

Questions 6-9.

DIRECTIONS: Answer Questions 6 to 9 ONLY according to the information given in the following passag

MOPPING FLOORS

When mopping hardened cement floors, either painted or unpainted, a soap and water mixture should be used. This should be made by dissolving 1/2 a cup of soft soap in a pail of hot water. It is not desirable, however, under any circumstances, to use a soap and water mixture on cement floors that are not hardened. For mopping this type of floor, it is recommended that the cleaning agent be made up of two ounces of laundry soda mixed in a pail of water.

Soaps are not generally used on hard tile floors because slippery films may build up on the floor. It is generally recommended that these floors be mopped using a pail of hot water in which has been mixed two ounces of washing powder for each gallon of water. The floors should then be rinsed thoroughly.

After the mopping is finished, proper care should be taken of the mop. This is done by first cleaning the mop in clear, warm water. Then, it should be wrung out, after which the strands of the mop should be untangled. Finally, the mop should be hung by its handle to dry.

6. According to the above passage, you should NEVER use a soap and water mixture when mopping _____ floors.   6.___

    A. hardened cement   B. painted
    C. unhardened cement   D. unpainted

7. According to the above passage, using laundry soda mixed in a pail of water as a cleaning agent is recommended for   7.___

    A. all floors
    B. all floors except hard tile floors
    C. some cement floors
    D. lineoleum floor coverings only

8. According to the above passage, the generally recommended mixture for mopping hard tile floors is   8.___

    A. 1/2 a cup of soft soap for each gallon of hot water
    B. 1/2 a cup of soft soap in a pail of hot water
    C. 2 ounces of washing powder in a pail of hot water
    D. 2 ounces of washing powder for each gallon of hot water

9. According to the above passage, the proper care of a mop after it is used includes　　9.＿＿＿

    A.　cleaning it in clear cold water and hanging it by its handle to dry
    B.　wringing it out, untangling and drying it
    C.　untangling its strands before wringing it out
    D.　untangling its strands while cleaning it in clear water

Questions 10-13.

DIRECTIONS:　Answer Questions 10 to 13 ONLY according to the information given in the following passage.

HANDLING HOSPITAL LAUNDRY

In a hospital, care must be taken when handling laundry in order to reduce the chance of germs spreading. There is always the possibility that dirty laundry will be carrying dangerous germs. To avoid catching germs when they are working with dirty laundry, laundry workers should be sure that any cuts or wounds they have are bandaged before they touch the dirty laundry. They should also be careful when handling this laundry not to rub their eyes, nose, or mout. Just like all other hospital workers, laundry workers should also protect themselves against germs by washing and rinsing their hands thoroughly before eating meals and before leaving work at the end of the day.

To be sure that germs from dirty laundry do not pass onto clean laundry and thereby increase the danger to patients, clean and dirty laundry should not be handled near each other or by the same person. Special care also has to be taken with laundry that comes from a patient who has a dangerous, highly contagious disease so that as few people as possible come in direct contact with this laundry. Laundry from this patient, therefore, should be kept separate from other dirty laundry at all times.

10.　According to the above passage, when working with dirty laundry, laundry workers should　　10.＿＿＿

    A.　destroy laundry carrying dangerous germs
    B.　have any cuts bandaged before touching the dirty laundry
    C.　never touch the dirty laundry directly
    D.　rub their eyes, nose, and mouth to protect them from germs

11.　According to the above passage, all hospital workers should wash their hands thoroughly　　11.＿＿＿

    A.　after eating meals to remove any trace of food from their hands
    B.　at every opportunity to show good example to the patients
    C.　before eating meals to protect themselves against germs
    D.　before starting work in the morning to feel fresh and ready to do a good day's work

12.　According to the above passage, the danger to patients will increase　　12.＿＿＿

    A.　unless a worker handles dirty and clean laundry at the same time
    B.　unless clean and dirty laundry are handled near each other
    C.　when clean laundry is ironed frequently
    D.　when germs pass from dirty laundry to clean laundry

13. According to the above passage, laundry from a patient with a dangerous, highly conta-   13.__
    gious disease should be

    A. given special care so that as few people as possible come in direct contact with it
    B. handled in the same way as any other dirty laundry
    C. washed by hand
    D. separated from the other dirty laundry just before it is washed

Questions 14-17.

DIRECTIONS: Answer Questions 14 to 17 ONLY according to the information given in the fol-
                lowing passage.

EMPLOYEE SUGGESTIONS

*To increase the effectiveness of the New York City governments the City asks its employ-
ees to offer suggestions when they feel an improvement could be made in some government
operation. The Employees' Suggestions Program was started to encourage City employees to
do this. Through this Program, which is only for City employees, cash awards may be given to
those whose suggestions are submitted and approve Suggestions are looked for not only from
supervisors but from all City employees as any City employee may get an idea which might be
approved and contribute greatly to the solution of some problem of City government.*

*Therefore, all suggestions for improvement are welcome, whether they be suggestions on
how to improve working conditions, or on how to increase the speed with which work is done, or
on how to reduce or eliminate such things as waste, time losses, accidents, or fire hazards.
There are, however, a few types of suggestions for which cash awards can not be given. An
example of this type would be a suggestion to increase salaries or a suggestion to change the
regulations about annual leave or about sick leave. The number of suggestions sent in has
increased sharply during the past few years. It is hoped that it will keep increasing in the future
in order to meet the City's needs for more ideas for improved ways of doing things.*

14. According to the above passage, the main reason why the City asks its employees for   14.__
    suggestions about government operations is to

    A. increase the effectiveness of the City government
    B. show that the Employees' Suggestion Program is working well
    C. show that everybody helps run the City government
    D. have the employee win a prize

15. According to the above passage, the Employees' Suggestion Program can approve   15.__
    awards only for those suggestions that come from

    A. City employees
    B. City employees who are supervisors
    C. City employees who are not supervisors
    D. experienced employees of the City

16. According to the above passage, a cash award can not be given through the Employees' Suggestion Program for a suggestion about   16._____

    A. getting work done faster
    B. helping prevent accidents on the job
    C. increasing the amount of annual leave for City employees
    D. reducing the chance of fire where City employees work

17. According to the above passage, the suggestions sent in during the past few years have   17._____

    A. all been approved
    B. generally been well written
    C. been mostly about reducing or eliminating waste
    D. been greater in number than before

Questions 18-21.

DIRECTIONS: Answer Questions 18 to 21 ONLY according to the information given in the following passage.

ACCIDENT PREVENTION

Many accidents and injuries can be prevented if employees learn to be more careful. The wearing of shoes with thin or badly worn soles or open toes can easily lead to foot injuries from tacks, nails, and chair and desk legs. Loose or torn clothing should not be worn near moving machinery. This is especially true of neckties which can very easily become caught in the machine. You should not place objects so that they block or partly block hallways, corridors, or other passageways. Even when they are stored in the proper place, tools, supplies, and equipment should be carefully placed or piled so as not to fall, nor have anything stick out from a pile. Before cabinets, lockers, or ladders are moved, the tops should be cleared of anything which might injure someone or fall of If necessary, use a dolly to move these or other bulky objects.

Despite all efforts to avoid accidents and injuries, however, some will happen. If an employee is injured, no matter how small the injury, he should report it to his supervisor and have the injury treated. A small cut that is not attended to can easily become infected and can cause more trouble than some injuries which at first seem more serious. It never pays to take chances.

18. According to the above passage, the one statement that is NOT true is that   18._____

    A. by being more careful, employees can reduce the number of accidents that happen
    B. women should wear shoes with open toes for comfort when working
    C. supplies should be piled so that nothing is sticking out from the pile
    D. if an employee sprains his wrist at work, he should tell his supervisor about it

19. According to the above passage, you should NOT wear loose clothing when you are   19._____

    A. in a corridor   B. storing tools
    C. opening cabinets   D. near moving machinery

20. According to the above passage, before moving a ladder, you should

    A. test all the rungs
    B. get a dolly to carry the ladder at all times
    C. remove everything from the top of the ladder which might fall off
    D. remove your necktie

20.__

21. According to the above passage, an employee who gets a slight cut should

    A. have it treated to help prevent infection
    B. know that a slight cut becomes more easily infected than a big cut
    C. pay no attention to it as it can't become serious
    D. realize that it is more serious than any other type of injury

21.__

Questions 22-24.

DIRECTIONS: Answer Questions 22 to 24 ONLY according to the information given in the following passage.

GOOD EMPLOYEE PRACTICES

As a City employee, you will be expected to take an interest in your work and perform the duties of your job to the best of your ability and in a spirit of cooperation. Nothing shows an interest in your work more than coming to work on time, not only at the start of the day but also when returning from lunch. If it is necessary for you to keep a personal appointment at lunch hour which might cause a delay in getting back to work on time, you should explain the situation to your supervisor and get his approval to come back a little late before you leave for lunch.

You should do everything that is asked of you willingly and consider important even the small jobs that your supervisor gives you. Although these jobs may seem unimportant, if you forget to do them or if you don't do them right, trouble may develop later.

Getting along well with your fellow workers will add much to the enjoyment of your work. You should respect your fellow workers and try to see their side when a disagreement arises. The better you get along with your fellow workers and your supervisor, the better you will like your job and the better you will be able to do it.

22. According to the above passage, in your job as a City employee, you are expected to

    A. show a willingness to cooperate on the job
    B. get your supervisor's approval before keeping any personal appointments at lunch hour
    C. avoid doing small jobs that seem unimportant
    D. do the easier jobs at the start of the day and the more difficult ones later on

22.__

23. According to the above passage, getting to work on time shows that you

    A. need the job
    B. have an interest in your work
    C. get along well with your fellow workers
    D. like your supervisor

23.__

24. According to the above passage, the one of the following statements that is NOT true is   24.____
    A. if you do a small job wrong, trouble may develop
    B. you should respect your fellow workers
    C. if you disagree with a fellow worker, you should try to see his side of the story
    D. the less you get along with your supervisor, the better you will be able to do your job

Questions 25-35.   <u>VOCABULARY</u>

25. The porter cleaned the VACANT room.   25.____
    In this sentence, the word VACANT means nearly the same as

    A. empty   B. large   C. main   D. crowded

26. The supervisor gave a BRIEF report to his men.   26.____
    In this sentence, the word BRIEF means nearly the same as

    A. long   B. safety   C. complete   D. short

27. The supervisor told him to CONNECT the two pieces.   27.____
    In this sentence, the word CONNECT means nearly the same as

    A. join   B. paint   C. return   D. weigh

28. Standing on the top of a ladder is RISKY.   28.____
    In this sentence, the word RISKY means nearly the same as

    A. dangerous   B. sensible   C. safe   D. foolish

29. He RAISED the cover of the machine.   29.____
    In this sentence, the word RAISED means nearly the same as

    A. broke   B. lifted   C. lost   D. found

30. The form used for reporting the finished work was REVISED.   30.____
    In this sentence, the word REVISED means nearly the same as

    A. printed   B. ordered   C. dropped   D. changed

31. He did his work RAPIDLY.   31.____
    In this sentence, the word RAPIDLY means nearly the same as

    A. carefully   B. quickly   C. slowly   D. quietly

32. The worker was OCCASIONALLY late   32.____
    In this sentence, the word OCCASIONALLY means nearly the same as

    A. sometimes   B. often   C. never   D. always

33. He SELECTED the best tool for the job.   33.____
    In this sentence, the word SELECTED means nearly the same as

    A. bought   B. picked   C. lost   D. broke

34. He needed ASSISTANCE to lift the package.   34.__
   In this sentence, the word ASSISTANCE means nearly the same as

   A. strength   B. time   C. help   D. instructions

35. The tools were ISSUED by the supervisor.   35.__
   In this sentence, the word ISSUED means nearly the same as

   A. collected   B. cleaned up
   C. given out   D. examined

———

KEY (CORRECT ANSWERS)

1.	C		16.	C
2.	B		17.	D
3.	C		18.	B
4.	B		19.	D
5.	A		20.	C
6.	C		21.	A
7.	C		22.	A
8.	D		23.	B
9.	B		24.	D
10.	B		25.	A
11.	C		26.	D
12.	D		27.	A
13.	A		28.	A
14.	A		29.	B
15.	A		30.	D

31.	B
32.	A
33.	B
34.	C
35.	C

———

READING COMPREHENSION
UNDERSTANDING AND INTERPRETING WRITTEN MATERIAL
EXAMINATION SECTION

DIRECTIONS: Each question or incomplete statement is followed by several suggested answers or completions. Select the one that BEST answers the question or completes the statement. *PRINT THE LETTER OF THE CORRECT ANSWER IN THE SPACE AT THE RIGHT.*

TEST 1

Questions 1-3.

DIRECTIONS: Questions 1 through 3 are to be answered SOLELY on the basis of the following paragraph.

Accident proneness is a subject which deserves much more objective and competent study than it has received to date. In discussing accident proneness, it is important to differentiate between the employee who is a *repeater* and one who is truly accident-prone. It is obvious that any person put on work of which he knows little without thorough training in safe practice for the work in question will be liable to injury until he does learn the *how* of it. Few workmen left to their own devices will develop adequate safe practices. Therefore, they must be trained. Only those who fail to respond to proper training should be regarded as accident-prone. The repeater whose accident record can be explained by a correctible physical defect, by correctible plant or machine hazards, by assignment to work for which he is not suited because of physical deficiencies or special abilities, cannot be fairly called *accident prone.*

1. According to the above paragraph, a person is considered accident prone if
   A. he has accidents regardless of the fact that he has been properly trained
   B. he has many accidents
   C. it is possible for him to have accidents
   D. he works at a job where accidents are possible

1.____

2. According to the above paragraph,
   A. workers will learn the safe way of doing things if left to their own intelligence
   B. most workers must be trained to be safe
   C. a worker who has had more than one accident has not been properly trained
   D. intelligent workers are always safe

2.____

3. According to the above paragraph, a person would not be called accident prone if the cause of his accident was
   A. a lack of interest in the job
   B. recklessness
   C. a low level of intelligence
   D. eyeglasses that don't fit properly

3.____

Questions 4-9.

DIRECTIONS: Each question consists of a statement. You are to indicate whether the statement is TRUE (T) or FALSE (F). Questions 4 through 9 are to be answered SOLELY on the basis of the following passage.

Every accident should be reported even though the accident seems very unimportant. The man involved may be unharmed, yet it is necessary in the case of all accidents to forward a written report containing all the facts that show how the accident occurred, including the time and place. The reason for this action is that a situation which does not cause injury at one time may cause serious injury at another time. A written report informs the safety director of a dangerous condition and helps his investigation by supplying important facts. He can, therefore, take steps to eliminate the hazard

4. Only serious accidents should be reported. 4.___

5. If the man involved in an accident is unharmed, it is not necessary to send through a report. 5.___

6. An accident report should show how the accident happened and include the time and place of the accident. 6.___

7. A situation which does not cause an injury at one time cannot cause serious injury at another time. 7.___

8. When a written report of an accident is made, it means that the safety director is informed of a dangerous condition. 8.___

9. The facts in an accident report do not help the safety director in his investigation of the accident. 9.___

Questions 10-17.

DIRECTIONS: Each question consists of a statement. You are to indicate whether the statement is TRUE (T) or FALSE (F). Questions 10 through 17 are to be answered SOLELY on the basis of the following passage.

The Mayor is in charge of the city government. He has his office in City Hall in downtown. There are city rules, or laws, that all citizens must obey. For example, there is a law that no one can throw things on the sidewalks or into the streets. We want our city to be clean and beautiful. There are also traffic laws for the automobiles that use our city streets. For instance, the cars cannot go at more than a certain speed. The drivers must stop when the traffic lights turn red.

If people do not obey these rules or city laws, a policeman may arrest them. These laws were made to protect other people who want to use the streets too.

10. The head of the city government is the Mayor.   10.___

11. The Mayor's office is in the Municipal Building.   11.___

12. The Mayor does not have to obey the city laws or rules.   12.___

13. Anyone who throws things on the sidewalks is breaking   13.___
     the law.

14. There is a traffic law that does not allow a car to go   14.___
     faster than a certain speed.

15. A driver does not have to stop when the traffic lights   15.___
     turn red.

16. A policeman may arrest a driver who does not obey the   16.___
     traffic laws.

17. People who use the streets are not protected by the   17.___
     traffic laws.

Questions 18-25.

DIRECTIONS: Each question consists of a statement. You are to
              indicate whether the statement is TRUE (T) or FALSE (F).
              Questions 18 through 25 are to be answered SOLELY on the
              basis of the following passage.

NEW YORK CITY

     The name of New York City, as it appears on all official documents,
is *The City of New York*. This name applies to all five boroughs which
consolidated in 1898 to form what is known as Greater New York. The
five boroughs are Manhattan, The Bronx, Brooklyn, Queens, and Richmond.
The term Greater New York is seldom used at the present time, and
often the city is called New York City to distinguish it from New York
State.

     The two Boroughs of Brooklyn and Queens are located on Long Island
and the Borough of Richmond is located on Staten Island. The Borough
of Manhattan is located on Manhattan Island, while The Bronx is
located on the mainland of New York State.

     Because the city is large, covers much territory, and has so many
people, the United States Post Office has divided the city for its own
convenience; therefore, the post office address of people living in
Manhattan is New York, New York. For those living in the Borough of
Brooklyn, the post office address is Brooklyn, New York; and, likewise,
each borough has its own special post office address.

18. New York City is referred to on all official documents as   18.___
     Greater New York City.

19. The boroughs of New York City were joined together in 1898   19.___
     to make up Greater New York.

20. Greater New York is made up of five boroughs.   20.____

21. The boroughs which make up New York City are The Bronx,   21.__
    Richmond, Brooklyn, Queens, and Nassau.

22. The borough of Queens is located on the mainland of New   22.____
    York State.

23. The Bronx and Brooklyn are part of Long Island.   23.____

24. A letter for Manhattan should be addressed to New York,   24.____
    New York.

25. Because New York City is so big, the Post Office has   25.____
    divided it into five different post office addresses.

TEST 2

Questions 1-4.

DIRECTIONS: Questions 1 through 4 are to be answered SOLELY on the
              basis of the following passage.

In the long run, a government will always encroach upon freedom
to the extent which it has the power to do so; this is almost a
natural law of politics since, whatever the intentions of the men
who exercise political power, the sheer momentum of government leads
to a constant pressure upon the liberties of the citizen. But in
many countries, society has responded by throwing up its own defenses
in the shape of social classes or organized corporations which, enjoy-
ing economic power and popular support, have been able to set limits
to the scope of action of the executive. Such, for example, in
England was the origin of all our liberties - won from government by
the stand first of the feudal nobility, then of churches and political
parties, and latterly of trade unions, commercial organizations, and
the societies for promoting various causes. Even European lands which
were arbitrarily ruled by the powers of the monarchy, though absolute
in theory, were in their exercise checked in a similar fashion. Indeed
the fascist dictatorships of today are the first truly tyrannical
governments which western Europe has known for centuries, and they
have been rendered possible only because on coming to power they
destroyed all forms of social organization which were in any way
rivals to the state.

1. The MAIN idea of the above passage is BEST expressed as   1.____
   A. limited powers of monarchies
   B. the ideal of liberal government
   C. functions of trade unions
   D. ruthless ways of dictators

2. The writer maintains that there is a natural tendency for governments to
    A. become more democratic
    B. become fascist
    C. increase individual liberties
    D. assume more power

    2.___

3. Monarchy was FIRST checked in England by the
    A. trade unions   B. church
    C. people   D. nobles

    3.___

4. Fascist dictatorships differ from monarchies of recent times in
    A. getting things done by sheer momentum
    B. promoting various causes
    C. exerting constant pressure on liberties
    D. destroying people's organizations

    4.___

Questions 5-8.

DIRECTIONS: Questions 5 through 8 are to be answered SOLELY on the basis of the following paragraph.

    Very early on a summer's morning, the nicest thing to look at is a beach, before the swimmers arrive. Usually all the litter has been picked up from the sand by the Park Department clean-up crew. Everything is quiet. All you can hear are the waves breaking and the sea gulls calling to each other. The beach opens to the public at 10 A.M. Long before that time, however, long lines of eager men, women, and children have driven up to the entrance. They form long lines that wind around the beach waiting for the signal to move.

5. According to the above paragraph, before 10 A.M., long lines are formed that are made up of
    A. cars   B. clean-up crews
    C. men, women, and children D. Park Department trucks

    5.___

6. The season referred to in the above paragraph is
    A. fall   B. summer   C. winter   D. spring

    6.___

7. The place the above paragraph is describing is a
    A. beach   B. park
    C. golf course   D. tennis court

    7.___

8. According to the above paragraph, one of the things you notice early in the morning is that
    A. radios are playing   B. swimmers are there
    C. the sand is dirty   D. the litter is gone

    8.___

Questions 9-10.

DIRECTIONS: Questions 9 and 10 are to be answered SOLELY on the basis of the following passage.

There have been almost as many definitions of *opinion* as there have been students of the problem, and the definitions have ranged from such a statement as *inconsistent views capable of being accepted by rational minds as true* to the *overt manifestation of an attitude*. There are, however, a number of clearly outstanding factors among the various definitions which form the sum total of the concept. Opinion is the stronghold of the individual. No *group* ever had an opinion, and there is no mechanism except that of the individual mind capable of forming an opinion. It is true, of course, that opinions can be altered or even created by the stimuli of environment. In the midst of individual diversity and confusion, every question as it rises into importance is subjected to a process of consolidation and clarification until there emerge certain views, each held and advocated in common by bodies of citizens. When a group of people accepts the same opinion, that opinion is public with respect to the group accepting it. When there is not unanimous opinion, there is not one public but two or more.

9. On the basis of the above passage, it may be INFERRED that 9.___
   A. all individual opinions are subjected to consolidation by the influence of environmental stimuli
   B. governments are influenced by opinions held in common by large groups of citizens
   C. some of the elements of the extremely varied definitions of *opinion* are compatible
   D. when there is no unanimity, there is no public opinion

10. On the basis of the above passage, the MOST accurate of 10.___
    the following statements is:
    A. One definition of *opinion* implies that most individuals can accept inconsistent views on the same question
    B. One other definition of *opinion* implies that the individual's attitude concerning a question must be openly expressed before it can be considered as an opinion
    C. The individual opinion plays no part in the stand taken on a given question by a group after the individual has identified himself with the group
    D. There are no group opinions formed on relatively unimportant issues because of individual confusion

Questions 11-13.

DIRECTIONS: Questions 11 through 13 are to be answered SOLELY on the basis of the following passage.

The word *propaganda* has fallen on evil days. As far as popular usage is concerned, its reputation by now is probably lost irretrievably, for its connotation is almost invariably sinister or evil. This is a pity for, in the struggle for men's minds, it is a weapon of great potential value. Indeed, in the race against time that we are running, its constructive use is indispensable. The student of propaganda must know that it is a term honorable in origin.

Propaganda is *good* or *bad* according to the virtue of the end to which it seeks to persuade us, and the methods it employs. Bad propaganda is distinguished by a disregard for the welfare of those at whom it is directed. Such disregard either derives from, or eventually results in, a lack of proper reverence for individuality, for the private person and our relation to him. For *man* is substituted *mass*, and the mass is manipulated for selfish purposes. The authoritarian reformist who believes he is acting *in the interest* of the masses is also involved in this same disregard for personal integrity. Its final outcome is always the same - a disregard for the individual. Good propaganda involves the deliberate avoidance of all casuistry. In so far as good propaganda operates upon us at a level of our weakness or disability, its intent must be to contribute a cure, not a sedative; inspiration, not an opiate; enlightenment, not accentuation of our ignorance.

11. Of the following, the MOST suitable title for the above passage is
    A. PROPAGANDA AND SOCIETY
    B. PROPAGANDA FOR THE MASSES
    C. THE PROPER MEANING OF PROPAGANDA
    D. USES AND MISUSES OF PROPAGANDA

11.___

12. On the basis of the above passage, it may be INFERRED that
    A. some propaganda may employ unscrupulous methods to persuade us to ends that are justified
    B. the definition of the word *propaganda* has been changed
    C. the method of frequent repetition is an example of bad propaganda
    D. the opportunity for the individual to challenge propaganda has decreased

12.___

13. On the basis of the above passage, it may be INFERRED THAT
    A. a reformer who believes in his cause should not employ propaganda to advance it
    B. good propaganda should be limited to operating against the levels of weakness of the individual
    C. propaganda may lose sight of the welfare of the individual in its appeal to the masses
    D. those who have privileged access to the media of mass communication must always accept high standards in their use of propaganda

13.___

Questions 14-15.

DIRECTIONS: Questions 14 and 15 are to be answered SOLELY on the basis of the following passage.

A steadfast concert for peace can never be maintained except by a partnership of democratic nations. No autocratic government could be trusted to keep faith within it or observe its covenants. It must be a league of honor, a partnership of opinion. Intrigue would eat its vitals away; the plottings of inner circles who could plan what

they would, and render account to no one, would be a corruption
seated at its very heart. Only free people can hold their purpose
and their honor steady to a common end, and prefer the interests
of mankind to any narrow interest of their own.

14. According to the above paragraph, only democratic nations   14.___
     can
         A. be free of plotting, intrigue, and corruption
         B. be trusted to do what is right and honorable
         C. plan programs which promote the interests of their
            country
         D. subordinate their own interests to those which benefit
            the entire world

15. It may be implied from the above passage that an autocratic 15.___
     government could NOT be trusted to respect its international
     agreements because it
         A. exemplifies the proverb that there is no honor among
            thieves
         B. is full of corruption, plots, and intrigue
         C. is principally concerned with the welfare of its own
            people
         D. would plot with other governments to advance their
            own mutual interests

Questions 16-17.

DIRECTIONS: Questions 16 and 17 are to be answered SOLELY on the
             basis of the following passage.

     A gentleman is mainly occupied in removing the obstacles which
hinder the free and unembarrassed action of those about him; and he
concurs with their movements rather than takes the initiative him-
self. The true gentleman carefully avoids whatever may cause a jar
or jolt in the minds of those with whom he is cast. His great con-
cern is to put everyone at his ease and to make all feel at home.
He is tender towards the bashful, gentle towards the distant, and
merciful towards the absurd; he can recollect to whom he is speaking;
he guards against unseasonable allusions, or topics which may irri-
tate; he is seldom prominent in conversation, and never wearisome.

16. According to the above passage, a gentleman makes it his   16.___
     business to
         A. discuss current issues of interest although contro-
            versial
         B. get the bashful to participate in the conversation
         C. introduce to one another guests who have not previously
            met
         D. remember the person with whom he is speaking

17. According to the above passage, one of the CHIEF charac-   17.___
     teristics of a gentleman is that he
         A. conducts himself in such a way as to avoid hurting
            the feelings of others
         B. keeps the conversation going, particularly when
            interest flags

C. puts an unruly guest in his place politely but firmly
D. shows his guests the ways in which they can best enjoy themselves

18. Too often we retire people who are willing and able to continue working, according to Federal Security Agency Administrator Oscar R. Ewing in addressing the first National Conference on Aging, to point up the fact that chronological age is no longer an effective criterion in determining whether or not an individual is capable of working. The Second World War proved this point when it became necessary to hire older, experienced people to handle positions in business and industry vacated by personnel called to serve their country. As shown by production records set during the war period, the employment of older people helped us continue, and even better, our high level of production.
It was also pointed out at the conference that our life expectancy is increasing and that the over-65 group will jump from 11,500,000 now to twenty million in 1985. A good many of these people are capable of producing and have a desire to work, but they are kept from gainful employment by a shortsightedness on the part of many employers which leads them to believe that young people alone can give them adequate service. It is true that the young person has greater agility and speed to offer, but on the other hand there is much to be gained from the experience, steadfastness, and maturity of judgment of the elderly worker.
The title that BEST expresses the ideas of the above passage is
    A. INCREASED EFFICIENCY OF ELDERLY WORKERS
    B. MISJUDGING ELDERLY WORKERS
    C. LENGTHENING THE SPAN OF LIFE
    D. NEW JOBS FOR THE AGED

18.____

19. The question is whether night baseball will prove a boon or a disaster to the game. The big crowds now attending the night games, the brilliance of the spectacle, the miracle of the spinning turnstiles - all these seem sufficient evidence that what is needed is not less night ball,but more. The fact remains, however, that despite all apparent success, some of the shrewdest, most experienced men in baseball remain unconvinced of the miracle. They are steady in their preference for daytime baseball, and they view with increasing distrust the race towards more lights. It could be that these men are simply being obstinate. Yet, on the other hand, it could be that in reviewing the caliber of baseball as it is played at night, in speculating upon the future effect of night ball, they are not entirely unprophetic. It could even be, indeed, that they are dead right.
In his attitude toward the future of night baseball, the author expresses
    A. uncertainty   B. confidence
    C. optimism   D. sharp criticism

19.____

20. We all know people who would welcome a new American car   20.____
    to their stables, but one cannot expect to find a sports-
    car man among them. He cannot be enticed into such a
    circus float without feeling soiled. He resents the wanton
    use of chromium as much as he shudders at the tail fins,
    the grotesquely convoluted bumpers, and other *dishonest*
    lines. He blanches at the enormous bustle that adds weight
    and useless space, drags on ramps and curbstones, and
    complicates the process of parking even in the car's own
    garage. The attitude of the owner of a Detroit product is
    reflected in the efforts of manufacturers to *take the drive*
    out of driving. The sportscar addict regards this stand as
    outrageous. His interest in a car, he is forever telling
    himself and other captive listeners, lies in the fun of
    driving it, in *sensing its alertness on the road*, and in
    pampering it as a thoroughbred.
    The above passage implies that sportscars are very
       A. colorful   B. showy
       C. maneuverable   D. roomy

Questions 21-25.

DIRECTIONS: Questions 21 through 25 are to be answered SOLELY on
               the basis of the following passage.

    Fuel is conserved when a boiler is operating near its most effi-
cient load. The efficiency of a boiler will change as the output
varies. Large amounts of air must be used at low ratings and so the
heat exchanger is inefficient. As the output increases, the efficiency decreases due to an increase in flue gas temperature. Every
boiler has an output rate for which its efficiency is highest. For
example, in a water-tube boiler, the highest efficiency might occur
at 120 percent of rated capacity while in a vertical fire-tube boiler
highest efficiency might be at 70% of rated capacity. The type of
fuel burned and cleanliness affects the maximum efficiency of the
boiler. When a power plant contains a battery of boilers, a sufficient number should be kept in operation so as to maintain the output
of individual units near their points of maximum efficiency. One of
the boilers in the battery can be used as a regulator to meet the
change in demand for steam while the other boilers could still operate
at their most efficient rating. Boiler performance is expressed as
the number of pounds of steam generated per pound of fuel.

21. According to the above paragraph, the number of pounds of   21.____
    steam generated per pound of fuel is a measure of boiler
       A. size   B. performance
       C. regulator input   D. by-pass

22. According to the above paragraph, the HIGHEST efficiency   22.____
    of a vertical fire tube boiler might occur at ____ capacity.
       A. 70% of rate   B. 80% of water tube
       C. 95% of water tube   D. 120% of rated

23. According to the above paragraph, the MAXIMUM efficiency   23.__
    of a boiler is affected by
       A. atmospheric temperature   B. atmospheric pressure
       C. cleanliness   D. fire brick material

24. According to the above paragraph, a heat exchanger uses   24.___
    large amounts of air at low
        A. fuel rates   B. ratings
        C. temperatures   D. pressures

25. According to the above paragraph, one boiler in a battery   25.___
    of boilers should be used as a
        A. demand   B. stand-by   C. regulator   D. safety

TEST 3

Questions 1-7.

DIRECTIONS: Questions 1 through 7 are to be answered SOLELY on the
              basis of the following paragraph on FIRST AID INSTRUCTIONS.

FIRST AID INSTRUCTIONS

The main purpose of first aid is to put the injured person in
the best possible position until medical help arrives. This includes
the performance of emergency treatment designed to save a life if a
doctor is not immediately available. When an accident happens, a
crowd usually collects around the victim. If nobody uses his head,
the injured person fails to receive the care he needs. You must keep
calm and cool at all times and, most important, it is your duty to
take charge at an accident. The first thing for you to do is to see,
insofar as possible, what is wrong with the injured person. Leave
him where he is until the nature and extent of his injury are determined. If he is unconscious, he should not be moved except to lay
him flat on his back if he is in some other position. Loosen the
clothing of any seriously hurt person, and make him as comfortable
as possible. Medical help should be called as soon as possible. You
should remain with the injured person and send someone else to call
the doctor. You should try to make sure that the one who calls for
a doctor is able to give correct information as to the location of the
injured person. In order to help the physician to know what equipment
may be needed in each particular case, the person making the call
should give the doctor as much information about the injury as possible.

1. If nobody uses his head at the scene of an accident, there   1.___
   is danger that
       A. a large crowd will gather
       B. emergency treatment will be needed
       C. names of witnesses will be missed
       D. the victim will not get the care he needs

2. The FIRST thing you should do at the scene of an accident   2.___
   is to
       A. call a doctor
       B. lay the injured person on his back
       C. find out what is wrong with the injured person
       D. loosen the clothing of the injured person

11

3. Until the nature and extent of the injuries are determined, 3.____
   you should
   A. move the injured person indoors
   B. let the injured person lie where he is
   C. carefully roll the injured person on his back
   D. give the injured person artificial respiration

4. If the injured person is unconscious, you should 4.____
   A. give him artificial respiration
   B. get some hot liquid like coffee into him
   C. lay him flat on his back
   D. move him to a comfortable location

5. If a doctor is to be called, you should 5.____
   A. go make this call yourself since you have all the
      information
   B. go make this call yourself since you are in charge
   C. send someone who knows what happened
   D. send someone who is fast

6. The person calling the doctor should give as much informa- 6.____
   tion as he has regarding the injury so that the doctor
   A. can bring the necessary equipment
   B. can decide whether he should come
   C. will know whom to notify
   D. can advise what should be done

7. The MAIN purpose of first aid is to 7._
   A. stop bleeding
   B. prevent further complications of the injury
   C. keep the patient comfortable
   D. determine what the injuries are

Questions 8-13.

DIRECTIONS: Questions 8 through 13 are to be answered SOLELY on
the basis of the following passage regarding selection
of tours of duty.

SELECTION OF TOURS OF DUTY

A selection of tours of duty for the winter season for Railroad
Porters will begin on Monday, December 27, and conclude on Thursday,
December 30.

The selection will take place in Room 828, 8th Floor, 370 Jay
Street, Telephone Elmer 2-5000, Extension 3870.

Railroad Porters whose names appear on the attached schedule
will make selections at the time and date indicated.

8. The selection of tours of duty began on 8.____
   A. Monday   B. Tuesday   C. Wednesday   D. Thursday

9. No selections of tours of duty were scheduled for December   9.___
    A. 28   B. 29   C. 30   D. 31

10. The choice of tours of duty was PROBABLY based on   10.___
    A. age
    B. seniority
    C. borough of residence
    D. alphabetical listing of names

11. The season for which the selection of tours of duty was made was the   11.___
    A. spring   B. summer   C. autumn   D. winter

12. A porter making a selection had to do so   12.___
    A. before work   B. after work
    C. on his day off   D. at the time indicated

13. The selecting was to be done by   13.___
    A. all station employees
    B. all porters
    C. only the porters whose names were on the schedule
    D. employees not satisfied with present schedules

Questions 14-16.

DIRECTIONS: Questions 14 through 16 are to be answered SOLELY on the basis of the following passage concerning car inspection and cleaning information.

RIGID INSPECTION: Subway cars are hauled into a repair yard and given a rigid inspection about three times a month.

SWEEPING AND WASHING: Each car is swept every twenty-four hours. Its windows are washed every time it comes into a repair yard.

OVERHAUL: At the completion of 90,000 miles, the car is almost completely taken apart, cleaned, and painted.

14. Car windows are USUALLY washed at least once in   14.___
    A. one day   B. three days
    C. ten days   D. three months

15. If the average car travelled about 75,000 miles per year, it would NORMALLY be almost completely taken apart, cleaned, and painted about every   15.___
    A. 9 months   B. year
    C. 15 months   D. 2 years

16. If a car has been overhauled at the end of 90,000 miles, it would be brought back to the repair yard   16.___
    A. within one week for sweeping
    B. within two weeks for another overhaul
    C. after 90,000 miles for inspection if necessary
    D. within two weeks for a rigid inspection

Questions 17-19.

DIRECTIONS: Questions 17 through 19 are to be answered SOLELY on the basis of the following passage.

Into the nine square miles that make up Manhattan's business districts, about two million people travel each weekday to go to work - the equivalent of the combined populations of Boston, Baltimore, and Cincinnati. Some 140,000 drive there in cars, 200,000 take buses, and 100,000 ride the commuter railroads. The great majority, however, go by subway - approximately 1.4 million people.

It is some ride. The last major improvement in the subway system was completed in 1935. The subways are dirty and noisy. Many local lines operate well beneath capacity, but many express lines are strained way beyond capacity - in particular, the lines to Manhattan, now overloaded by 39,000 passengers during peak hours.

But for all its discomforts, the subway system is inherently a far more efficient way of moving people than automobiles and highways. Making this system faster, more convenient, and more comfortable for people must be the core of the City's transportation effort.

17. The CENTRAL point of the above passage is that   17.____
    A. the equivalent of the combined populations of Boston, Baltimore, and Cincinnati commute into Manhattan's business district each weekday
    B. the improvement of the subway system is the key to the solution of moving people efficiently in and out of Manhattan's business district
    C. the subways are dirty and noisy, resulting in a terrible ride
    D. we should increase the ability of people to get in and out of Manhattan by cars, subways, and commuter railroads in order to ease the load from the subways

18. In accordance with the above passage, 1.4 million people   18.____
    commute by subway and _____ by other mass transportation means.
    A. 200,000   B. 100,000   C. 440,000   D. 300,000

19. From the information given in the above passage, one   19.____
    could logically conclude that, next to the subways, the transportation system that carries the LARGEST number of passengers is
    A. railroads   B. cars
    C. buses   D. local lines

Questions 20-25.

DIRECTIONS: Questions 20 through 25 are to be answered SOLELY on the basis of the following passage. Each question consists of a statement. You are to indicate whether the statement is TRUE (T) or FALSE (F).

THE CITY

The City, which at one time in 1789-90 was the capital of the nation and which was also the capital of the State until 1796, has continued as the financial and economic capital of the United States and has grown to be the greatest city in the country.

The City is great because it has such a large population - a total of eight million persons in 1988. This population is larger than the total inhabitants of 41 of 75 of the largest countries in the world. The City requires many homes and buildings to accommodate its residents. The City consists of more than 725,000 buildings, more than half of which are one and two family houses owned by the occupants. More than five hundred hotels, with 128,000 rooms, are needed to take care of the visitors to the City; it is estimated that between one and two hundred thousand people visit the City daily.

The harbor is so large that any six of the other leading seaports of the world could be placed in it. Its piers, to accommodate freight and passengers, number 471, and its waterfront covers 770 miles.

20. The City has been the capital of the United States and also the capital of the State.   20.____

21. In 1988, the population of the City was greater than the total population of forty-one of seventy-five of the largest countries in the world.   21.____

22. Over half of all the buildings in the City are one and two family homes which are owned by the people who live in them.   22.____

23. A little under 200,000 people visit the City each year.   23.____

24. The harbor is larger than any other leading seaport.   24.____

25. The harbor is 471 miles long and has 770 piers to take care of passengers and cargo.   25.____

15

KEY (CORRECT ANSWERS)

TEST 1

1. A
2. B
3. D
4. F
5. F

6. T
7. F
8. T
9. F
10. T

11. F
12. F
13. T
14. T
15. F

16. T
17. F
18. F
19. T
20. T

21. F
22. F
23. F
24. T
25. T

TEST 2

1. D
2. D
3. D
4. D
5. C

6. B
7. A
8. D
9. C
10. B

11. D
12. A
13. C
14. D
15. D

16. D
17. A
18. B
19. A
20. C

21. B
22. A
23. C
24. B
25. C

TEST 3

1. D
2. C
3. B
4. C
5. C

6. A
7. B
8. A
9. D
10. B

11. D
12. D
13. C
14. C
15. C

16. D
17. B
18. D
19. C
20. T

21. T
22. T
23. F
24. T
25. F

CLERICAL ABILITIES

EXAMINATION SECTION
TEST 1

DIRECTIONS: Each question or incomplete statement is followed by several suggested answers or completions. Select the one that BEST answers the question or completes the statement. *PRINT THE LETTER OF THE CORRECT ANSWER IN THE SPACE AT THE RIGHT.*

Questions 1-4.

DIRECTIONS: Questions 1 through 4 are to be answered on the basis of the information given below.

The most commonly used filing system and the one that is easiest to learn is alphabetical filing. This involves putting records in an A to Z order, according to the letters of the alphabet. The name of a person is filed by using the following order: first, the surname or last name; second, the first name; third, the middle name or middle initial. For example, *Henry C. Young* is filed under *Y* and thereafter under *Young, Henry C.* The name of a company is filed in the same way. For example, *Long Cabinet Co.* is filed under *L*, while *John T. Long Cabinet Co.* is filed under *L* and thereafter under *Long., John T. Cabinet Co.*

1. The one of the following which lists the names of persons in the CORRECT alphabetical order is:

    A. Mary Carrie, Helen Carrol, James Carson, John Carter
    B. James Carson, Mary Carrie, John Carter, Helen Carrol
    C. Helen Carrol, James Carson, John Carter, Mary Carrie
    D. John Carter, Helen Carrol, Mary Carrie, James Carson

1.____

2. The one of the following which lists the names of persons in the CORRECT alphabetical order is:

    A. Jones, John C.; Jones, John A.; Jones, John P.; Jones, John K.
    B. Jones, John P.; Jones, John K.; Jones, John C.; Jones, John A.
    C. Jones, John A.; Jones, John C.; Jones, John K.; Jones, John P.
    D. Jones, John K.; Jones, John C.; Jones, John A.; Jones, John P.

2.____

3. The one of the following which lists the names of the companies in the CORRECT alphabetical order is:

    A. Blane Co., Blake Co., Block Co., Blear Co.
    B. Blake Co., Blane Co., Blear Co., Block Co.
    C. Block Co., Blear Co., Blane Co., Blake Co.
    D. Blear Co., Blake Co., Blane Co., Block Co.

3.____

4. You are to return to the file an index card on *Barry C. Wayne Materials and Supplies Co.* Of the following, the CORRECT alphabetical group that you should return the index card to is

    A. A to G   B. H to M   C. N to S   D. T to Z

4.____

Questions 5-10.

DIRECTIONS: In each of Questions 5 through 10, the names of four people are given. For each question, choose as your answer the one of the four names given which should be filed FIRST according to the usual system of alphabetical filing of names, as described in the following paragraph.

In filing names, you must start with the last name. Names are filed in order of the first letter of the last name, then the second letter, etc. Therefore, BAILY would be filed before BROWN, which would be filed before COLT. A name with fewer letters of the same type comes first; i.e., Smith before Smithe. If the last names are the same, the names are filed alphabetically by the first name. If the first name is an initial, a name with an initial would come before a first name that starts with the same letter as the initial. Therefore, I. BROWN would come before IRA BROWN. Finally, if both last name and first name are the same, the name would be filed alphabetically by the middle name, once again an initial coming before a middle name which starts with the same letter as the initial. If there is no middle name at all, the name would come before those with middle initials or names.

Sample Question:
A. Lester Daniels
B. William Dancer
C. Nathan Danzig
D. Dan Lester

The last names beginning with D are filed before the last name beginning with L. Since DANIELS, DANCER, and DANZIG all begin with the same three letters, you must look at the fourth letter of the last name to determine which name should be filed first. C comes before I or Z in the alphabet, so DANCER is filed before DANIELS or DANZIG. Therefore, the answer to the above sample question is B.

5.
A. Scott Biala
B. Mary Byala
C. Martin Baylor
D. Francis Bauer

5.____

6.
A. Howard J. Black
B. Howard Black
C. J. Howard Black
D. John H. Black

6.____

7.
A. Theodora Garth Kingston
B. Theadore Barth Kingston
C. Thomas Kingston
D. Thomas T. Kingston

7.____

8.
A. Paulette Mary Huerta
B. Paul M. Huerta
C. Paulette L. Huerta
D. Peter A. Huerta

8.____

9. A. Martha Hunt Morgan
    B. Martin Hunt Morgan
    C. Mary H. Morgan
    D. Martine H. Morgan

10. A. James T. Meerschaum
    B. James M. Mershum
    C. James F. Mearshaum
    D. James N. Meshum

Questions 11-14.

DIRECTIONS: Questions 11 through 14 are to be answered SOLELY on the basis of the following information.

You are required to file various documents in file drawers which are labeled according to
the following pattern:

DOCUMENTS

MEMOS		LETTERS	
File	Subject	File	Subject
84PM1	- (A-L)	84PC1	- (A-L)
84PM2	- (M-Z)	84PC2	- (M-Z)

REPORTS		INQUIRIES	
File	Subject	File	Subject
84PR1	- (A-L)	84PQ1	- (A-L)
84PR2	- (M-Z)	84PQ2	- (M-Z)

11. A letter dealing with a burglary should be filed in the drawer labeled

   A. 84PM1   B. 84PC1   C. 84PR1   D. 84PQ2

12. A report on Statistics should be found in the drawer labeled

   A. 84PM1   B. 84PC2   C. 84PR2   D. 84PQ2

13. An inquiry is received about parade permit procedures. It should be filed in the drawer
    labeled

   A. 84PM2   B. 84PC1   C. 84PR1   D. 84PQ2

14. A police officer has a question about a robbery report you filed.
    You should pull this file from the drawer labeled

   A. 84PM1   B. 84PM2   C. 84PR1   D. 84PR2

Questions 15-22.

DIRECTIONS: Each of Questions 15 through 22 consists of four or six numbered names. For
each question, choose the option (A, B, C, or D) which indicates the order in
which the names should be filed in accordance with the following filing instructions:
   - File alphabetically according to last name, then first name, then middle initial.
   - File according to each successive letter within a name.

- When comparing two names in which, the letters in the longer name are identical to the corresponding letters in the shorter name, the shorter name is filed first.
- When the last names are the same, initials are always filed before names beginning with the same letter.

15. I.   Ralph Robinson
    II. Alfred Ross
    III. Luis Robles
    IV. James Roberts
The CORRECT filing sequence for the above names should be

  A. IV, II, I, III   B. I, IV, III, II
  C. III, IV, I, II   D. IV, I, III, II

16. I.   Irwin Goodwin
    II. Inez Gonzalez
    III. Irene Goodman
    IV. Ira S. Goodwin
    V.   Ruth I. Goldstein
    VI. M.B. Goodman
The CORRECT filing sequence for the above names should be

  A. V, II, I, IV, III, VI   B. V, II, VI, III, IV, I
  C. V, II, III, VI, IV, I   D. V, II, III, VI, I, IV

17. I.   George Allan
    II. Gregory Allen
    III. Gary Allen
    IV. George Allen
The CORRECT filing sequence for the above names should be

  A. IV, III, I, II   B. I, IV, II, III
  C. III, IV, I, II   D. I, III, IV, II

18. I.   Simon Kauffman
    II. Leo Kaufman
    III. Robert Kaufmann
    IV. Paul Kauffmann
The CORRECT filing sequence for the above names should be

  A. I, IV, II, III   B. II, IV, III, I
  C. III, II, IV, I   D. I, II, III, IV

19. I.   Roberta Williams
    II. Robin Wilson
    III. Roberta Wilson
    IV. Robin Williams
The CORRECT filing sequence for the above names should be

  A. III, II, IV, I   B. I, IV, III, II
  C. I, II, III, IV   D. III, I, II, IV

20.
    I.   Lawrence Shultz
    II. Albert Schultz
    III. Theodore Schwartz
    IV. Thomas Schwarz
    V. Alvin Schultz
    VI. Leonard Shultz

The CORRECT filing sequence for the above names should be

A. II, V, III, IV, I, VI
C. II, V, I, VI, III, IV

B. IV, III, V, I, II, VI
D. I, VI, II, V, III, IV

20.____

21.
    I.   McArdle
    II. Mayer
    III. Maletz
    IV. McNiff
    V. Meyer
    VI. MacMahon

The CORRECT filing sequence for the above names should be

A. I, IV, VI, III, II, V
C. VI, III, II, I, IV, V

B. II, I, IV, VI, III, V
D. VI, III, II, V, I, IV

21.____

22.
    I.   Jack E. Johnson
    II. R.H. Jackson
    III. Bertha Jackson
    IV. J.T. Johnson
    V. Ann Johns
    VI. John Jacobs

The CORRECT filing sequence for the above names should be

A. II, III, VI, V, IV, I
C. VI, II, III, I, V, IV

B. III, II, VI, V, IV, I
D. III, II, VI, IV, V, I

22.____

Questions 23-30.

DIRECTIONS: The code table below shows 10 letters with matching numbers. For each question, there are three sets of letters. Each set of letters is followed by a set of numbers which may or may not match their correct letter according to the code table. For each question, check all three sets of letters and numbers and mark your answer:

    A. if no pairs are correctly matched
    B. if only one pair is correctly matched
    C. if only two pairs are correctly matched
    D. if all three pairs are correctly matched

CODE TABLE

T	M	V	D	S	P	R	G	B	H
1	2	3	4	5	6	7	8	9	0

Sample Question: TMVDSP - 123456
                       RGBHTM - 789011
                       DSPRGB - 256789

In the sample question above, the first set of numbers correctly matches its set of letters. But the second and third pairs contain mistakes. In the second pair, M is incorrectly matched with number 1. According to the code table, letter M should be correctly matched with number 2. In the third pair, the letter D is incorrectly matched with number 2. According to the code table, letter D should be correctly matched with number 4. Since only one of the pairs is correctly matched, the answer to this sample question is B.

23. RSBMRM 759262   23._____
    GDSRVH 845730
    VDBRTM 349713

24. TGVSDR 183247   24._____
    SMHRDP 520647
    TRMHSR 172057

25. DSPRGM 456782   25._____
    MVDBHT 234902
    HPMDBT 062491

26. BVPTRD 936184   26._____
    GDPHMB 807029
    GMRHMV 827032

27. MGVRSH 283750   27._____
    TRDMBS 174295
    SPRMGV 567283

28. SGBSDM 489542   28._____
    MGHPTM 290612
    MPBMHT 269301

29. TDPBHM 146902   29._____
    VPBMRS 369275
    GDMBHM 842902

30. MVPTBV 236194   30._____
    PDRTMB 647128
    BGTMSM 981232

KEY (CORRECT ANSWERS)

1.	A	11.	B	21.	C
2.	C	12.	C	22.	B
3.	B	13.	D	23.	B
4.	D	14.	D	24.	B
5.	D	15.	D	25.	C
6.	B	16.	C	26.	A
7.	B	17.	D	27.	D
8.	B	18.	A	28.	A
9.	A	19.	B	29.	D
10.	C	20.	A	30.	A

TEST 2

DIRECTIONS: Each question or incomplete statement is followed by several suggested answers or completions. Select the one that BEST answers the question or completes the statement. *PRINT THE LETTER OF THE CORRECT ANSWER IN THE SPACE AT THE RIGHT.*

Questions 1-10.

DIRECTIONS: Questions 1 through 10 each consists of two columns, each containing four lines of names, numbers and/or addresses. For each question, compare the lines in Column I with the lines in Column II to see if they match exactly, and mark your answer A, B, C, or D, according to the following instructions:
   A.   all four lines match exactly
   B.   only three lines match exactly
   C.   only two lines match exactly
   D.   only one line matches exactly

	COLUMN I	COLUMN II	
1.	I. Earl Hodgson II. 1409870 III. Shore Ave. IV. Macon Rd.	Earl Hodgson 1408970 Schore Ave. Macon Rd.	1.____
2.	I. 9671485 II. 470 Astor Court III. Halprin, Phillip IV. Frank D. Poliseo	9671485 470 Astor Court Halperin, Phillip Frank D. Poliseo	2.____
3.	I. Tandem Associates II. 144-17 Northern Blvd. III. Alberta Forchi IV. Kings Park, NY 10751	Tandom Associates 144 17 Northern Blvd. Albert Forchi Kings Point, NY 10751	3.____
4.	I. Bertha C. McCormack II. Clayton, MO. III. 976-4242 IV. New City, NY 10951	Bertha C. McCormack Clayton, MO. 976-4242 New City, NY 10951	4.____
5.	I. George C. Morill II. Columbia, SC 29201 III. Louis Ingham IV. 3406 Forest Ave.	George C. Morrill Columbia, SD 29201 Louis Ingham 3406 Forest Ave.	5.____
6.	I. 506 S. Elliott P1. II. Herbert Hall III. 4712 Rockaway Pkway IV. 169 E. 7 St.	506 S. Elliott P1. Hurbert Hall 4712 Rockaway Pkway 169 E. 7 St.	6.____

	COLUMN I	COLUMN II	

7.

I.	345 Park Ave.	345 Park P1.
II.	Colman Oven Corp.	Coleman Oven Corp.
III.	Robert Conte	Robert Conti
IV.	6179846	6179846

7._____

8.

I.	Grigori Schierber	Grigori Schierber
II.	Des Moines, Iowa	Des Moines, Iowa
III.	Gouverneur Hospital	Gouverneur Hospital
IV.	91-35 Cresskill P1.	91-35 Cresskill P1.

8._____

9.

I.	Jeffery Janssen	Jeffrey Janssen
II.	8041071	8041071
III.	40 Rockefeller Plaza	40 Rockafeller Plaza
IV.	407 6 St.	406 7 St.

9._____

10.

I.	5971996	5871996
II.	3113 Knickerbocker Ave.	3113 Knickerbocker Ave.
III.	8434 Boston Post Rd.	8424 Boston Post Rd.
IV.	Penn Station	Penn Station

10._____

Questions 11-14.

DIRECTIONS: Questions 11 through 14 are to be answered by looking at the four groups of names and addresses listed below (I, II, III, and IV) and then finding out the number of groups that have their corresponding numbered lines exactly the same.

	GROUP I	GROUP II
Line 1.	Richmond General Hospital	Richman General Hospital
Line 2.	Geriatric Clinic	Geriatric Clinic
Line 3.	3975 Paerdegat St.	3975 Peardegat St.
Line 4	Loudonville, New York 11538	Londonville, New York 11538

	GROUP III	GROUP IV
Line 1.	Richmond General Hospital	Richmend General Hospital
Line 2.	Geriatric Clinic	Geriatric Clinic
Line 3.	3795 Paerdegat St.	3975 Paerdegat St.
Line 4.	Loudonville, New York 11358	Loudonville, New York 11538

11. In how many groups is line one exactly the same?   11._____

    A. Two   B. Three   C. Four   D. None

12. In how many groups is line two exactly the same?   12._____

    A. Two   B. Three   C. Four   D. None

13. In how many groups is line three exactly the same?   13._____

    A. Two   B. Three   C. Four   D. None

14. In how many groups is line four exactly the same?   14.__

    A. Two   B. Three   C. Four   D. None

Questions 15-18.

DIRECTIONS: Each of Questions 15 through 18 has two lists of names and addresses. Each list contains three sets of names and addresses. Check each of the three sets in the list on the right to see if they are the same as the corresponding set in the list on the left. Mark your answers:
    A. if none of the sets in the right list are the same as those in the left list
    B. if only one of the sets in the right list is the same as those in the left list
    C. if only two of the sets in the right list are the same as those in the left list
    D. if all three sets in the right list are the same as those in the left list

15.   Mary T. Berlinger   Mary T. Berlinger   15.____
        2351 Hampton St.   2351 Hampton St.
        Monsey, N.Y. 20117   Monsey, N.Y. 20117

        Eduardo Benes   Eduardo Benes
        473 Kingston Avenue   473 Kingston Avenue
        Central Islip, N.Y. 11734   Central Islip, N.Y. 11734

        Alan Carrington Fuchs 17 Gnarled   Alan Carrington Fuchs 17 Gnarled
        Hollow Road Los Angeles, CA   Hollow Road Los Angeles, CA
        91635   91685

16.   David John Jacobson   David John Jacobson   16.____
        178 35 St. Apt. 4C   178 53 St. Apt. 4C
        New York, N.Y. 00927   New York, N.Y. 00927

        Ann-Marie Calonella   Ann-Marie Calonella
        7243 South Ridge Blvd.   7243 South Ridge Blvd.
        Bakersfield, CA 96714   Bakersfield, CA 96714

        Pauline M. Thompson   Pauline M. Thomson 872 Linden
        872 Linden Ave. Houston,   Ave. Houston, Texas 70321
        Texas 70321

17.   Chester LeRoy Masterton   Chester LeRoy Masterson   17.____
        152 Lacy Rd.   152 Lacy Rd.
        Kankakee, 111. 54532   Kankakee, 111. 54532

        William Maloney   William Maloney
        S. LaCrosse Pla.   S. LaCross Pla.
        Wausau, Wisconsin 52146   Wausau, Wisconsin 52146

        Cynthia V. Barnes   Cynthia V. Barnes
        16 Pines Rd.   16 Pines Rd.
        Greenpoint, Miss. 20376   Greenpoint, Miss. 20376

18.
Marcel Jean Frontenac	Marcel Jean Frontenac	
8 Burton On The Water	6 Burton On The Water	
Calender, Me. 01471	Calender, Me. 01471	18._____
J. Scott Marsden	J. Scott Marsden	
174 S. Tipton St.	174 Tipton St.	
Cleveland, Ohio	Cleveland, Ohio	
Lawrence T. Haney	Lawrence T. Haney	
171 McDonough St.	171 McDonough St.	
Decatur, Ga. 31304	Decatur, Ga. 31304	

Questions 19-26.

DIRECTIONS: Each of Questions 19 through 26 has two lists of numbers. Each list contains three sets of numbers. Check each of the three sets in the list on the right to see if they are the same as the corresponding set in the list on the left. Mark your answers:

    A.   if none of the sets in the right list are the same as those in the left list

    B.   if only one of the sets in the right list is the same as those in the left list

    C.   if only two of the sets in the right list are the same as those in the left list

    D.   if all three sets in the right list are the same as those in the left list

19.   7354183476   7354983476   19._____
       4474747744   4474747774
       57914302311   57914302311

20.   7143592185   7143892185   20._____
       8344517699   8344518699
       9178531263   9178531263

21.   2572114731   257214731   21._____
       8806835476   8806835476
       8255831246   8255831246

22.   331476853821   331476858621   22._____
       6976658532996   6976655832996
       3766042113715   3766042113745

23.   8806663315   8806663315   23._____
       74477138449   74477138449
       211756663666   211756663666

24.   990006966996   99000696996   24._____
       53022219743   53022219843
       4171171117717   4171171177717

25.   24400222433004   24400222433004   25._____
       5300030055000355   5300030055500355
       20000075532002022   20000075532002022

26. 611166640660001116   61116664066001116   26.__
    711300117001100733   711300117001100733
    26666446664476518   26666446664476518

Questions 27-30.

DIRECTIONS: Questions 27 through 30 are to be answered by picking the answer which is in the correct numerical order, from the lowest number to the highest number, in each question.z

27. A. 44533, 44518, 44516, 44547   27.____
    B. 44516, 44518, 44533, 44547
    C. 44547, 44533, 44518, 44516
    D. 44518, 44516, 44547, 44533

28. A. 95587, 95593, 95601, 95620   28.____
    B. 95601, 95620, 95587, 95593
    C. 95593, 95587, 95601, 95620
    D. 95620, 95601, 95593, 95587

29. A. 232212, 232208, 232232, 232223   29.____
    B. 232208, 232223, 232212, 232232
    C. 232208, 232212, 232223, 232232
    D. 232223, 232232, 232208, 232212

30. A. 113419, 113521, 113462, 113588   30.__
    B. 113588, 113462, 113521, 113419
    C. 113521, 113588, 113419, 113462
    D. 113419, 113462, 113521, 113588

KEY (CORRECT ANSWERS)

1. C	11. A	21. C
2. B	12. C	22. A
3. D	13. A	23. D
4. A	14. A	24. A
5. C	15. C	25. C
6. B	16. B	26. C
7. D	17. B	27. B
8. A	18. B	28. A
9. D	19. B	29. C
10. C	20. B	30. D

EXAMINATION SECTION
TEST 1

DIRECTIONS: Each question or incomplete statement is followed by several suggested
                     answers or completions. Select the one that *BEST* answers the question or
                     completes the statement. *PRINT THE LETTER OF THE CORRECT ANSWER
                     IN THE SPACE AT THE RIGHT.*

Questions 1-5.

DIRECTIONS: Each question from 1 to 5 consists of a sentence with an underlined word. For
                     each question, select the choice that is *CLOSEST* in meaning to the under-
                     lined word.

EXAMPLE
This division reviews the fiscal reports of the agency.
In this sentence the word *fiscal* means most nearly
   A.   financial   B.   critical   C.   basic   D.   personnel
The correct answer is A. "financial" because "financial"
is closest to *fiscal.* Therefore, the answer is A.

1.   Every good office worker needs basic skills.   1._____
     The word *basic* in this sentence means

        A.   fundamental   B.   advanced   C.   unusual   D.   outstanding

2.   He turned out to be a good instructor.   2._____
     The word *instructor* in this sentence means

        A.   student   B.   worker   C.   typist   D.   teacher

3.   The quantity of work in the office was under study.   3._____
     In this sentence, the word *quantity* means

        A.   amount   B.   flow   C.   supervision   D.   type

4.   The morning was spent examining the time records.   4._____
     In this sentence, the word *examining* means

        A.   distributing   B.   collecting   C.   checking   D.   filing

5.   The candidate filled in the proper spaces on the form.   5._____
     In this sentence, the word *proper* means

        A.   blank   B.   appropriate   C.   many   D.   remaining

Questions 6-8.

DIRECTIONS: You are to answer Questions 6 through 8 *SOLELY* on the basis of the informa-
                     tion contained in the following paragraph:
     The increase in the number of public documents in the last two centuries closely matches
the increase in population in the United States. The great number of public documents has
become a serious threat to their usefulness. It is necessary to have programs which will reduce
the number of public documents that are kept and which will, at the same time, assure keeping
those that have value. Such programs need a great deal of thought to have any success.

6. According to the above paragraph, public documents may be less useful if   6.____

   A. the files are open to the public
   B. the record room is too small
   C. the copying machine is operated only during normal working hours
   D. too many records are being kept

7. According to the above paragraph, the growth of the population in the United States has matched the growth in the quantity of public documents for a period of, most nearly,   7.____

   A. 50 years   B. 100 years   C. 200 years   D. 300 years

8. According to the above paragraph, the increased number of public documents has made it necessary to   8.____

   A. find out which public documents are worth keeping
   B. reduce the great number of public documents by decreasing government services
   C. eliminate the copying of all original public documents
   D. avoid all new copying devices.

Questions 9-10.

DIRECTIONS: You are to answer Questions 9 and 10 *SOLELY* on the basis of the information contained in the following paragraph:

The work goals of an agency can best be reached if the employees understand and agree with these goals. One way to gain such understanding and agreement is for management to encourage and seriously consider suggestions from employees in the setting of agency goals.

9. On the basis of the paragraph above, the *BEST* way to achieve the work goals of an agency is to   9.____

   A. make certain that employees work as hard as possible
   B. study the organizational structure of the agency
   C. encourage employees to think seriously about the agency's problems
   D. stimulate employee understanding of the work goals

10. On the basis of the paragraph above, understanding and agreement with agency goals can be gained by   10.____

   A. allowing the employees to set agency goals
   B. reaching agency goals quickly
   C. legislative review of agency operations
   D. employee participation in setting agency goals

Questions 11-15.

DIRECTIONS: Each of Questions 11 through 15 consists of a group of four words. One word in each group is *INCORRECTLY* spelled. For each question, print the letter of the correct answer in the space at the right that is the same as the letter next to the word which is *INCORRECTLY* spelled.
EXAMPLE
   A. housing   B. certain   C. budgit   D. money

The word "budgit" is incorrectly spelled, because the correct spelling should be "budget." Therefore, the correct answer is C.

11. A. sentince   B. bulletin   C. notice   D. definition   11.____
12. A. appointment   B. exactly   C. typest   D. light   12.____
13. A. penalty   B. suparvise   C. consider   D. division   13.____
14. A. schedule   B. accurate   C. corect   D. simple   14.____
15. A. suggestion   B. installed   C. proper   D. agincy   15.____

Questions 16-20.

DIRECTIONS: Each question from 16 through 20 consists of a sentence which may be
    A. incorrect because of bad word usage, or
    B. incorrect because of bad punctuation, or
    C. incorrect because of bad spelling, or
    D. correct
Read each sentence carefully. Then print in the proper space at the right A, B, C, or D, according to the answer you choose from the four choices listed above. There is only one type of error in each incorrect sentence. If there is no error, the sentence is correct.

EXAMPLE

George Washington was the father of his contry.
This sentence is incorrect because of bad spelling ("contry" instead of "country"). Therefore, the answer is C.

16. The assignment was completed in record time but the payroll for it has not yet been pre-parid.   16.____

17. The operator, on the other hand, is willing to learn me how to use the mimeograph.   17.____

18. She is the prettiest of the three sisters.   18.____

19. She doesn't know; if the mail has arrived.   19.____

20. The doorknob of the office door is broke.   20.____

21. A clerk can process a form in 15 minutes. How many forms can that clerk process in six hours?   21.____

    A. 10   B. 21   C. 24   D. 90

22. An office staff consists of 120 people. Sixty of them have been assigned to a special project. Of the remaining staff, 20 answer the mail, 10-handle phone calls, and the rest operate the office machines. The number of people operating the office machines is   22.____

    A. 20   B. 30   C. 40   D. 45

23. An office worker received 65 applications but on the first day had to return 26 of them for being incomplete and on the second day 25 had to be returned for being incomplete. How many applications did <u>not</u> have to be returned?   23.____

    A. 10   B. 12   C. 14   D. 16

24. An office worker answered 63 phone calls in one day and 91 phone calls the next day. For these 2 days, what was the average number of phone calls he answered per day?   24.____

   A. 77   B. 28   C. 82   D. 93

25. An office worker processed 12 vouchers of $8.75 each, 3 vouchers of $3.68 each, and 2 vouchers of $1.29 each. The total dollar amount of these vouchers is   25.____

   A. $116.04   B. $117.52   C. $118.62   D. $119.04

KEY (CORRECT ANSWERS)

1. A		11. A	
2. D		12. C	
3. A		13. B	
4. C		14. C	
5. B		15. D	
6. D		16. C	
7. C		17. A	
8. A		18. D	
9. D		19. B	
10. D		20. A	

21. C
22. B
23. C
24. A
25. C

TEST 2

DIRECTIONS: Each question or incomplete statement is followed by several suggested answers or completions. Select the one that *BEST* answers the question or completes the statement. *PRINT THE LETTER OF THE CORRECT ANSWER IN THE SPACE AT THE RIGHT.*

Questions 1-5.

DIRECTIONS: Each question from 1 to 5 lists four names. The names may or may not be exactly the same. Compare the names in each question and mark your answer as follows:

Mark your answer A if all the names are different
Mark your answer B if only two names are exactly the same
Mark your answer C if only three names are exactly the same
Mark your answer D if all four names are exactly the same

EXAMPLE
Jensen, Alfred E.
Jensen, Alfred E.
Jensan, Alfred E.
Jensen, Fred E.

Since the name Jensen, Alfred E. appears twice and is exactly the same in both places, the correct answer is B.

1. Riviera, Pedro S.
    Rivers, Pedro S.
    Riviera, Pedro N.
    Riviera, Juan S.
                  1.____

2. Guider, Albert
    Guidar, Albert
    Giuder, Alfred
    Guider, Albert
                  2.____

3. Blum, Rona
    Blum, Rona
    Blum, Rona
    Blum, Rona
                  3.____

4. Raugh, John
    Raugh, James
    Raughe, John
    Raugh, John
                  4.____

5. Katz, Stanley
    Katz, Stanley
    Katze, Stanley
    Katz, Stanley
                  5.____

Questions 6-10.

DIRECTIONS: Each Question 6 through 10 consists of numbers or letters in Columns I and II.
For each question, compare each line of Column I with its corresponding line
in Column II and decide how many lines in Column I are *EXACTLY* the same
as their corresponding lines in Column II. In your answer space, mark your
answer as follows:

Mark your answer A if only *ONE* line in Column I is exactly the
same as its corresponding line in Column II
Mark your answer B if only *TWO* lines in Column I are exactly the
same as their corresponding lines in Column II
Mark your answer C if only *THREE* lines in Column I are exactly
the same as their corresponding lines in Column II
Mark your answer D if all *FOUR* lines in Column I are exactly the same as their corresponding lines in Column II

EXAMPLE

Column I	Column II
1776	1776
1865	1865
1945	1945
1976	1978

Only three lines in Column I are exactly the same as their corresponding lines in Column II.
Therefore, the correct answer is C.

	Column I	Column II	
6.	5653	5653	6.___
	8727	8728	
	ZPSS	ZPSS	
	4952	9453	
7.	PNJP	PNPJ	7.___
	NJPJ	NJPJ	
	JNPN	JNPN	
	PNJP	PNPJ	
8.	effe	eFfe	8.___
	uWvw	uWvw	
	KpGj	KpGg	
	vmnv	vmnv	
9.	5232	5232	9.___
	PfrC	PfrN	
	zssz	zzss	
	rwwr	rwww	
10.	czws	czws	10.___
	cecc	cece	
	thrm	thrm	
	lwtz	lwtz	

Questions 11-15.

DIRECTIONS: Questions 11 through 15 have lines of letters and numbers. Each letter should be matched with its number in accordance with the following table:

Letter	F	R	C	A	W	L	E	N	P	T
Matching Number	0	1	2	3	4	5	6	7	8	9

From the table you can determine that the letter F has the matching number 0 below it, the letter R has the matching number 1 below it, etc.

For each question, compare each line of letters and numbers carefully to see if each letter has its correct matching number. If all the letters and numbers are matched correctly in

none of the lines of the question, mark your answer A
only one of the lines of the question, mark your answer B
only two of the lines of the question, mark your answer C
all three lines of the question, mark your answer D

EXAMPLE

WBCR	4826
TLBF	9580
ATNE	3986

There is a mistake in the first line because the letter R should riave its matching number 1 instead of the number 6.

The second line is correct because each letter shown has the correct matching number.

There is a mistake in the third line because the letter N should have the matching number 7 instead of the number 8,

Since all the letters and numbers are matched correctly in only one of the lines in the sample, the correct answer is B.

11.	EBCT	6829	11._____
	ATWR	3961	
	NLBW	7584	

12.	RNCT	1729	12._____
	LNCR	5728	
	WAEB	5368	

13.	NTWB	7948	13._____
	RABL	1385	
	TAEF	9360	

14.	LWRB	5417	14._____
	RLWN	1647	
	CBWA	2843	

15.	ABTC	3792	15._____
	WCER	5261	
	AWCN	3417	

16. Your job often brings you into contact with the public. Of the following, it would be *MOST* desirable to explain the reasons for official actions to people coming into your office for assistance because such explanations   16.___

    A. help build greater understanding between the public and your agency
    B. help build greater self-confidence in city employees
    C. convince the public that nothing they do can upset a city employee
    D. show the public that city employees are intelligent

17. Assume that you strongly dislike one of your co-workers.   17.___
You should *FIRST*

    A. discuss your feeling with the co-worker
    B. demand a transfer to another office
    C. suggest to your supervisor that the co-worker should be observed carefully
    D. try to figure out the reason for this dislike before you say or do anything

18. An office worker who has problems accepting authority is *MOST* likely to find it difficult to   18.___

    A. obey rules   B. understand people
    C. assist other employees   D. follow complex instructions

19. The employees in your office have taken a dislike to one person and frequently annoy her. Your supervisor *should*   19.___

    A. transfer this person to another unit at the first opportunity
    B. try to find out the reason for the staff's attitude before doing anything about it
    C. threaten to transfer the first person observed bothering this person
    D. ignore the situation

20. Assume that your supervisor has asked a worker in your office to get a copy of a report out of the files. You notice the worker has accidentally pulled out the wrong report. Of the following, the *BEST* way for you to handle this situation is to tell   20.___

    A. the worker about all the difficulties that will result from this error
    B. the worker about her mistake in a nice way
    C. the worker to ignore this error
    D. your supervisor that this worker needs more training in how to use the files

21. Filing systems differ in their efficiency. Which of the following is the *BEST* way to evaluate the efficiency of a filing system?   21.___
The

    A. number of times used per day
    B. amount of material that is received each day for filing
    C. amount of time it takes to locate material
    D. type of locking system used

22. In planning ahead so that a sufficient amount of general office supplies is always available, it would be *LEAST* important to find out the   22.___

    A. current office supply needs of the staff
    B. amount of office supplies used last year
    C. days and times that office supplies can be ordered
    D. agency goals and objectives

23. The *MAIN* reason for establishing routine office work procedures is that once a routine is established   23.____

    A. work need not be checked for accuracy
    B. all steps in the routine will take an equal amount of time to perform
    C. each time the job is repeated it will take less time to perform
    D. each step in the routine will not have to be planned all over again each time

24. When an office machine centrally located in an agency must be shut down for repairs, the bureaus and divisions using this machine should be informed of the   24.____

    A. expected length of time before the machine will be in operation again
    B. estimated cost of repairs
    C. efforts being made to avoid future repairs
    D. type of new equipment which the agency may buy in the future to replace the machine being repaired

25. If the day's work is properly scheduled, the *MOST* important result would be that the   25.____

    A. supervisor will not have to do much supervision
    B. employee will know what to do next
    C. employee will show greater initiative
    D. job will become routine

KEY (CORRECT ANSWERS)

1.	A		11.	C
2.	B		12.	B
3.	D		13.	D
4.	B		14.	B
5.	C		15.	A
6.	B		16.	A
7.	B		17.	D
8.	B		18.	A
9.	A		19.	B
10.	C		20.	B

21.	C
22.	D
23.	D
24.	A
25.	B

ARITHMETICAL REASONING
EXAMINATION SECTION
TEST 1

DIRECTIONS: Each question or incomplete statement is followed by several suggested answers or completions. Select the one that BEST answers the question or completes the statement. *PRINT THE LETTER OF THE CORRECT ANSWER IN THE SPACE AT THE RIGHT.*

Questions 1-4.

DIRECTIONS: Answer Questions 1 through 4 by performing the operation required (addition or subtraction).

1. Add: 10,487
        +   145   1.___

    A. 10,342   B. 10,622   C. 10,632   D. 10,652

2. Add: 26,836
        +   87   2.___

    A. 26,749   B. 26,923   C. 26,943   D. 26,973

3. Subtract: 83,204
             -83,075   3.___

    A. 109   B. 129   C. 139   D. 144

4. Subtract: 19,095
             -19,029   4.___

    A. 66   B. 74   C. 79   D. 86

5. If the mileage indicator on your truck reads 14,382 at   5.___
    the beginning of the day, and it reads 14,431 at the end
    of the day, the number of miles that the truck has been
    driven that day is
    A. 29   B. 34   C. 39   D. 49

6. On a certain day, your truck makes three trips to the   6.___
    dumping area and dumps 5.5 tons, 6.3 tons, and 4.8 tons
    of trash.
    The TOTAL number of tons of trash that the truck has
    dumped that day is
    A. 15.0   B. 15.6   C. 16.0   D. 16.6

7. During one winter, there were 29 snowfalls with a total   7.___
    snow accumulation for the season of 57.6 inches. The next
    winter, there were 15 snowfalls with a total snow accumu-
    lation for the season of 7.9 inches.
    The average snow accumulation per snowfall for the two
    winters combined was MOST NEARLY ____ inch(es).
    A. 1.00   B. 1.25   C. 1.50   D. 1.75

8. In District A, 1/6 of the sanitation work force took all   8.___
   its vacation in June, 1/3 of the force took all its
   vacation in July, and 1/4 took all its vacation in August.
   What part of the total sanitation work force of the
   district does this represent?
      A. 3/4   B. 7/12   C. 2/5   D. 3/13

9. In a four-year period, the Department of Sanitation used   9.___
   314,997 tons of salt for snow removal. The first year,
   79,651 tons were used. The second year, the Department
   used 6,592 tons less than the first year. In the third
   year, 11,981 tons of salt more were used than were used
   in the second year.
   The number of tons of salt used in the fourth year was
   MOST NEARLY
      A. 77,275   B. 77,250   C. 77,225   D. 77,200

10. Suppose that the number of occupancies that the Depart-   10.___
    ment of Sanitation collects from in 6 different sections
    of the city are, respectively, 1,837, 962, 12,105, 4,923,
    26,702, and 3,819.
    The total number of occupancies that the Department must
    collect from in these 6 sections is MOST NEARLY
       A. 50,355   B. 50,350   C. 50,345   D. 50,340

11. A rectangular box measures 6 feet by 2½ feet.   11.___
    If the box is 3 feet deep, the cubic volume of the box
    is MOST NEARLY _____ cubic inches.
       A. 78,000   B. 41,000   C. 4,500   D. 138

12. Following is a list of symbols and their meanings: 12.___
       DSL = average loads per hour received from Department
             of Sanitation
       DST = total tons per day received from Department of
             Sanitation
       OL = total loads per day received from others
       OT = average tons per hour received from others
    Based on the above, which one of the following formulas
    will give the average tons per load received at an
    incinerator plant?

    A. $\dfrac{(24xDSL + OL)}{(DST + 24xOT)}$ B. $\dfrac{(DST + OT)}{(24xDSL + OL)}$

    C. $\dfrac{(DST + 24xOT)}{(24xDSL + OL)}$ D. $\dfrac{DST + 24xOT}{24xDSL + 24xOL}$

13. Assume that you are required to assist in the evaluation   13.___
    of a new piece of sanitation equipment that is powered
    by a diesel engine. The following data are available to
    you: fuel consumption is 0.6 pounds of fuel per hour per
    horsepower, 40 horsepower is required to meet the load,
    the fuel weighs 7 pounds per gallon.
    Assuming 6 hours of operation per day, the number of
    gallons of fuel required is MOST NEARLY _____ gallons
    per day.
       A. 13   B. 20   C. 46   D. 100

14. Assume you are determining, from a large scale map ($\frac{1}{2}$ inch = $\frac{1}{4}$ mile), the number of curb miles per man day for a mechanical sweeper. As you measure map distance, your notes show 10 1/8 inches, 8 3/4 inches, and 7$\frac{1}{2}$ inches for the entire route. The total curb miles is MOST NEARLY

  A. 6.7   B. 13.2   C. 14.5   D. 18.1   14.____

15. The total area, in square feet, of the following rooms: 15.____

Room	Square Feet
201	1,196
202	1,196
203	827
204	827

is MOST NEARLY

  A. 3,000   B. 4,000   C. 5,000   D. 6,000

16. The AVERAGE area of the rooms listed in the preceding question is _____ of the total.   16.____

  A. 1/4   B. 1/3   C. 1/2   D. 3/4

17. The Public Relations Office's budget was $10,000.00 in 1992. Their 1993 budget was 5% higher than that of 1992, and their 1994 budget was 10% higher than that of 1993. The Office's budget for 1994 is   17.____

  A. $10,550   B. $11,150   C. $11,550   D. $12,050

18. The city recently purchased three pieces of machinery for use at a sanitation garage. One machine cost $1,739.55, the second machine cost $6,284.00. The total cost for all three machines was $12,721.00. How much did the third machine cost?   18.____

  A. $4,607.55   B. $4,697.45   B. $4,797.55   D. $4,798.45

19. An Emergency Sanitation Aide is paid at the rate of $7.20 per hour. He worked 45 hours in one week and was paid double time for 3 of the 45 hours worked during this week. What was his TOTAL gross earnings for the week?   19.____

  A. $336.90   B. $345.60   C. $378.90   D. $465.60

20. Assuming that it requires 6 man-days to replace a sidewalk 4 feet wide x 120 feet long, then a similar sidewalk 8 feet wide x 78 feet long would require MOST NEARLY _____ man-days.   20.____

  A. 6   B. 8   C. 10   D. 14

KEY (CORRECT ANSWERS)

1. C	6. D	11. A	16. A
2. B	7. C	12. C	17. C
3. B	8. A	13. B	18. B
4. A	9. B	14. B	19. B
5. D	10. B	15. B	20. B

SOLUTIONS TO PROBLEMS

1. $10,487 + 145 = 10,632$

2. $26,836 + 87 = 26,923$

3. $83,204 - 83,075 = 129$

4. $19,095 - 19,029 = 66$

5. $14,431 - 14,382 = 49$ miles

6. $5.5 + 6.3 + 4.8 = 16.6$ tons of trash

7. $(57.6+7.9) \div (29+15) \approx 1.50$ in. per snowfall

8. $\frac{1}{6} + \frac{1}{3} + \frac{1}{4} = \frac{9}{12} = \frac{3}{4}$

9. 4th year usage $= 314,997 - (79,651+73,059+85,040) = 77,247$, or about 77,250 tons of salt

10. $1837 + 962 + 12,105 + 4923 + 26,702 + 3819 = 50,348 \approx 50,350$

11. $(72")(30")(36") = 77,760$ cu.in. $\approx 78,000$ cu.in.

12. Average tons/load $= (DST+24 \cdot OT) \div (24 \cdot DSL+OL)$
    Note: $24 \cdot DSL$ = total loads per day received by DST
    $24 \cdot OT$ = total tons per day received by others

13. $(.6)(40)(6) = 144$. Then, $144 \div 7 \approx 20.57 \approx 20$ gallons

14. $10\frac{1}{8}" + 8\frac{3}{4}" + 7\frac{1}{2}" = 26\frac{3}{8}"$. Then, $26\frac{3}{8}" \div \frac{1}{2}" = 52.75$
    Finally, $(52.75)(\frac{1}{4}$ mi.$) \approx 13.2$ miles

15. $1196 + 1196 + 827 + 827 = 4046$ sq. ft. ≈ 4000 sq.ft.

16. $4046 \div 4 = 1011.5$, and 1011.5 must be $\frac{1}{4}$ of the total sq.ft.

17. For 1994, the budget was $(\$10,000)(1.05)(1.10) = \$11,550$

18. $\$12,721 - \$1739.55 - \$6284 = \$4697.45$

19. $(\$7.20)(42) + (\$14.40)(3) = \$345.60$

20. $(4')(120') = 480$ sq.ft., $(8')(78') = 624$ sq.ft. Then, we have
    $(6)(\frac{624}{480}) = 7.8 \approx 8$ man-days

———

TEST 2

1. If a section had 48 miles of street to plow after a snow-storm and 9 plows are used, each plow would cover an average of 4 miles.   1.____

2. If a crosswalk plow engine is run 5 minutes a day for ten days in a given month, it would run one hour in the course of this month.   2.____

3. If the department uses 1,500 men in manual street cleaning and half as many more to load and drive trucks, the total number used is 2,200 men.   3.____

4. If an inspector issued 186 summonses in the course of 7 hours, his hourly average was 25 summonses issued.   4.____

5. If an inspector issued 186 summonses, one hundred were issued to first offenders, then there were 86 summonses issued to other than first offenders.   5.____

6. If one length of hose is 50 feet, six lengths equal 250 feet.   6.____

7. If the Department has 2 officers to every 18 men, the ratio is 1 to 9.   7.____

8. A street measuring 200' by 36' from curb to curb has an area of 800 square yards.   8.____

9. A ton pick-up truck will hold at least 2,000 lbs.   9.____

10. An employee who works from 6 P.M. to 4 A.M. the following morning works a total of 8 hours.   10.____

11. A truck body measuring $5\frac{1}{2}$ feet by $1\frac{1}{2}$ feet by 8 feet has a capacity of 66 cubic feet.   11.____

12. A sanitation truck averaging 18 miles per hour travels approximately 6 miles in 20 minutes.   12.____

13. A sanitation man born July 20, 1928 was 21 years and 22 days old on August 11, 1949.   13.____

14. If 231 cubic inches equal one gallon, then a $2\frac{1}{2}$ gallon fire extinguisher measures about 577.5 cubic inches.   14.____

15. If a scraper costs $1.87, then 100 scrapers will cost   15.____
    $18.70.

16. A loaded truck weighs 5,400 pounds. If the truck weighs   16.____
    twice as much as the load, the load weighs 1,800 pounds.

17. If eight men are needed to sweep a particular area in   17.____
    6 hours, it would only take six men to sweep this area
    in 8 hours.

18. If a collection truck travels a half mile in 10 minutes,   18.____
    its speed is 15 miles per hour.

19. If twelve cans of sweepings fill a truck which can hold   19.____
    $1\frac{1}{2}$ tons, three cans of sweepings will fill a truck
    holding 1/2 ton.

20. The capacity of the body of a hired truck which is six   20.____
    feet wide, ten feet long, and six feet high is the same
    as one which measures six feet by twelve feet by five
    feet.

21. The sum of 2,345 and 4,483 is 6,882.   21.____

22. One-fifth of 295 is 59.   22.____

23. The difference between 2,876 and 1,453 is 1,423.   23.____

24. If each of 5 sections has 15 solar cans, the total of all   24.____
    five sections is 75 cans.

25. If there are 245 sections in the city, the average number   25.____
    of sections for each of the 5 counties is 49 sections.

26. If three men working at the same rate of speed finish a   26.____
    job in $4\frac{1}{2}$ hours, then two of them could do the job in
    6 3/4 hours.

27. If a typist shares four boxes of envelopes with four   27.____
    other typists, each will have one box of envelopes.

28. An article bought for $100 must be sold for $125 in order   28.____
    to make a profit of 20% of the selling price.

29. 1/2 of 1/8 is 1/4.   29.____

30. Ten square feet of carpet will cover the floor of a room   30.____
    10 feet by 10 feet.

———

KEY (CORRECT ANSWERS)

1.	F	11.	T	21.	F
2.	F	12.	T	22.	T
3.	F	13.	T	23.	T
4.	F	14.	T	24.	T
5.	T	15.	F	25.	T
6.	F	16.	T	26.	T
7.	T	17.	T	27.	F
8.	T	18.	F	28.	T
9.	T	19.	F	29.	F
10.	F	20.	T	30.	F

SOLUTIONS TO PROBLEMS

1. False. $48 \div 9 = 5\frac{1}{3} \approx 5$ miles, not 4 miles

2. False. $(5)(10) = 50$ min., not 1 hour

3. False. $1500 + (\frac{1}{2})(1500) = 2250$ men, not 2200 men

4. False. $186 \div 7 \approx 27$ summonses/hr., not 25 summonses/hr.

5. True. $186 - 100 = 86$ summonses

6. False. $(6)(50') = 300$ ft., not 250 ft.

7. True. 2:18 reduces to 1:9

8. True. $(200')(36') = 7200$ sq.ft. $= 800$ sq.yds. (1 sq.yd. = 9 sq.ft.)

9. True. 1 ton = 2000 lbs.

10. False. From 6 P.M. to 4 A.M. = 10 hrs., not 8 hrs.

11. True. $(5\frac{1}{2}')(1\frac{1}{2}')(8') = 66$ cu.ft.

12. True. 18 mi/hr is equivalent to 6 mi/$\frac{1}{3}$ hr = 6 mi/20 min

13. True. From 7/20/28 to 8/11/49 is 21 yrs. and 22 days

14. True. $(231)(2.5) = 577.5$ cu.in.

15. False. $(\$1.87)(100) = \$187$, not $18.70

16. True. Let x = wt. of load, 2x = wt. of truck. Then, 3x = 5400. Solving, x = 1800 lbs.

17. True. $(8)(6) = 48$ man-hours, so $48 \div 8 = 6$ men

18. False. $\frac{1}{2}$ mi. in 10 min. equals 3 mi/hr, not 15 mi/hr

19. False. $12 \div 3 = 4$, and $1\frac{1}{2} \div 4 = \frac{3}{8}$ ton, not $\frac{1}{2}$ ton

20. True. $(6')(10')(6') = 360$ cu.ft. $= (6')(12')(5')$

21. False. $2345 + 4483 = 6828$, not 6882

22. True. $(\frac{1}{5})(295) = 59$

23. True. 2876 - 1453 = 1423

24. True. (5)(15) = 75 cans

25. True. 245 ÷ 5 = 49 sections

26. True. (3)(4.5) = 13.5 man-hrs., so 13.5 ÷ 2 = 6.75 hrs.

27. False. 5 typists ÷ 4 boxes means each typist will have $\frac{4}{5}$ box, not 1 box

28. True. Profit = $125 - $100 = $25, and $25 ÷ $125 = 20%

29. False. $(\frac{1}{2})(\frac{1}{8}) = \frac{1}{16}$, not $\frac{1}{4}$

30. False. (10')(10') = 100 sq.ft., not 10 sq.ft.

———

TEST 3

DIRECTIONS: Each question consists of a statement. You are to indicate whether the statement is TRUE (T) or FALSE (F). *PRINT THE LETTER OF THE CORRECT ANSWER IN THE SPACE AT THE RIGHT.*

1. If the medical examiner is expected to arrive an hour and fifteen minutes past 9:28 A.M. and he comes 12 minutes later than that, then it is 10:45 A.M. when he arrives. 1.____

2. A city hearse going at a rate of 44 miles an hour should cover 4 miles in 11 minutes. 2.____

3. If 8% of the alcohol in a container has evaporated, then 23/25ths of the original amount is still there. 3.____

4. If a mortuary caretaker works 7 hours each day for 46 days, the total number of hours he has worked in these 46 days is 322. 4.____

5. If a person's weight has gone down from 120 pounds to 105 pounds, his weight has gone down by 11%. 5.____

6. If Mortuary A has 26 bodies and Mortuary B has 2 more than twice as many as Mortuary A, then Mortuary B has 29 bodies. 6.____

7. Adding up these numbers: 2,693, 264, 1,701, and 849 gives a total of 4,507. 7.____

8. If bodies A and B together weigh 375 lbs. and body A alone weighs 187 pounds, then body B must weigh 188 pounds. 8.____

9. If 16 mortuaries are going to share equally 144 boxes of supplies, then each mortuary should get 9 boxes of supplies. 9.____

10. If eleven bodies are delivered to the mortuary the first day, 8 the second day, and 5 the third day, then the average number of bodies delivered per day for this period is 7. 10.____

11. If a temperature of 98.6 degrees is normal, then a temperature of 103.2 degrees is 4.6 degrees above normal. 11.____

12. If a hospital with a bed capacity of 2,100 beds reports that 87% of its beds are occupied, then the number of beds not occupied is 373. 12.____

13. It takes a hospital clerk 8 minutes to prepare an admission report on one patient. At this rate, it will take the hospital clerk 5 hours and 36 minutes to prepare the admission reports on 42 patients. 13.____

14. Three-fifths of the patients in Hospital X are males.   14.___
    If the total number of patients in Hospital X is 1,550,
    then the number of male patients is 930.

15. In a certain hospital, requests for laboratory examina-   15.___
    tions are made out in duplicate on a special laboratory
    request form. The laboratory request forms are bound
    in pads, each pad containing 80 forms. If 480 laboratory
    examinations were requested during the month of November,
    the number of pads used in November was 6 pads.

16. Of 1,376 apartments in a public housing project, 868 are   16.___
    three-room apartments. Therefore, the number of apart-
    ments in this project that are not three-room apartments
    is 508.

17. Attendant A is working twice as fast as Attendant B;   17.___
    therefore, in the same period of time, Attendant B does
    one-half the amount of work that Attendant A does.

18. An attendant has cleaned a wall 14 feet long and 7 feet   18.___
    high; he has, therefore, cleaned 108 square feet of wall
    surface.

19. An employee is paid $4.00 an hour for the first 40 hours   19.___
    that he works in one week and $6.00 an hour for every
    hour that he works over 40 hours in a week; therefore,
    if he works 50 hours in one week, he will be paid $220.

20. Each of six windows in a children's shelter measures 3   20.___
    feet wide by 6 feet high; the total window space of these
    six windows is 126 square feet.

21. You are instructed to divide 1,092 paper towels equally   21.___
    among 14 people; therefore, you should give each person
    78 towels.

22. If two wheels of unequal size are rolled the same dis-   22.___
    tance across a floor, the smaller wheel will make less
    turns in this distance than the larger one.

23. An attendant who pays $9.13 each week for 49 weeks into   23.___
    a pension fund has, in this period of time, paid $447.37
    into this pension fund.

24. In the course of his duties, an attendant must find the   24.___
    answer to 50 times 80. Adding up a column of fifty
    eighties will give the same answer as multiplying eighty
    by fifty.

25. An attendant gave these directions to a man who asked for   25.___
a location in the city: *From 42nd Street and 8th Avenue,
walk one block west; turn right and walk one block; then
turn left and walk half a block, and you're at the place
you're looking for.* Following these directions would
place the man on 43rd Street.

KEY (CORRECT ANSWERS)

1. F		11. T
2. F		12. F
3. T		13. T
4. T		14. T
5. F		15. F
6. F		16. T
7. F		17. T
8. T		18. F
9. T		19. T
10. F		20. F
	21. T	
	22. F	
	23. T	
	24. T	
	25. T	

SOLUTIONS TO PROBLEMS

1. False. 9:28 A.M. + 1 hr. 15 min. + 12 min. = 10:55 A.M., not 10:45 A.M.

2. False. 44 mi/hr = 4 mi. in $\frac{60}{11}$ = 5.$\overline{45}$ min., not 11 min.

3. True. 100% − 8% = 92% = $\frac{23}{25}$

4. True. (7)(46) = 322 hrs.

5. False. 120 − 105 = 15 lbs., and $\frac{15}{120}$ = 12½%, not 11%

6. False. 2 + (2)(26) = 54, not 29

7. False. 2693 + 264 + 1701 + 849 = 5507, not 4507

8. True. 375 − 187 = 188 lbs.

9. True. 144 ÷ 16 = 9 boxes

10. False. (11+8+5) ÷ 3 = 8, not 7

11. True. 103.2° − 98.6° = 4.6°

12. False. 100% − 87% = 13%, and (13%)(2100) = 273, not 373

13. True. (8 min.)(42) = 336 min. = 5 hrs. and 36 min.

14. True. $(\frac{3}{5})$(1550) = 930 male patients

15. False. Each exam requires 2 forms, so a pad of 80 forms is sufficient for 40 exams. Then, 480 ÷ 40 = 12 pads, not 6 pads

16. True. 1376 − 868 = 508 apartments

17. True. Since attendant A is twice as fast as attendant B, B's work = ½ the amount of A's work (in the same time)

18. False. (14')(7') = 98 sq.ft., not 108 sq.ft.

19. True. ($4)(40) + ($6)(10) = $220

20. False. (6)(3')(6') = 108 sq.ft., not 126 sq.ft.

21. True.   1092 ÷ 14 = 78 towels

22. False. A smaller wheel will actually make more turns in going
     the same distance as a larger wheel.

23. True. ($9.13)(49) = $447.37

24. True. Adding fifty 80's = (50)(80) = 4000

25. True. 42nd St. + 1 block north = 43rd St.

———

ANSWER SHEET

TEST NO. ______________ PART ______ TITLE OF POSITION ______________________________
(AS GIVEN IN EXAMINATION ANNOUNCEMENT - INCLUDE OPTION, IF ANY)

PLACE OF EXAMINATION ______________________________ (CITY OR TOWN) ______________ (STATE) DATE ______________

RATING

USE THE SPECIAL PENCIL. MAKE GLOSSY BLACK MARKS.

1 A B C D E	26 A B C D E	51 A B C D E	76 A B C D E	101 A B C D E
2 A B C D E	27 A B C D E	52 A B C D E	77 A B C D E	102 A B C D E
3 A B C D E	28 A B C D E	53 A B C D E	78 A B C D E	103 A B C D E
4 A B C D E	29 A B C D E	54 A B C D E	79 A B C D E	104 A B C D E
5 A B C D E	30 A B C D E	55 A B C D E	80 A B C D E	105 A B C D E
6 A B C D E	31 A B C D E	56 A B C D E	81 A B C D E	106 A B C D E
7 A B C D E	32 A B C D E	57 A B C D E	82 A B C D E	107 A B C D E
8 A B C D E	33 A B C D E	58 A B C D E	83 A B C D E	108 A B C D E
9 A B C D E	34 A B C D E	59 A B C D E	84 A B C D E	109 A B C D E
10 A B C D E	35 A B C D E	60 A B C D E	85 A B C D E	110 A B C D E

Make only ONE mark for each answer. Additional and stray marks may be counted as mistakes. In making corrections, erase errors COMPLETELY.

11 A B C D E	36 A B C D E	61 A B C D E	86 A B C D E	111 A B C D E
12 A B C D E	37 A B C D E	62 A B C D E	87 A B C D E	112 A B C D E
13 A B C D E	38 A B C D E	63 A B C D E	88 A B C D E	113 A B C D E
14 A B C D E	39 A B C D E	64 A B C D E	89 A B C D E	114 A B C D E
15 A B C D E	40 A B C D E	65 A B C D E	90 A B C D E	115 A B C D E
16 A B C D E	41 A B C D E	66 A B C D E	91 A B C D E	116 A B C D E
17 A B C D E	42 A B C D E	67 A B C D E	92 A B C D E	117 A B C D E
18 A B C D E	43 A B C D E	68 A B C D E	93 A B C D E	118 A B C D E
19 A B C D E	44 A B C D E	69 A B C D E	94 A B C D E	119 A B C D E
20 A B C D E	45 A B C D E	70 A B C D E	95 A B C D E	120 A B C D E
21 A B C D E	46 A B C D E	71 A B C D E	96 A B C D E	121 A B C D E
22 A B C D E	47 A B C D E	72 A B C D E	97 A B C D E	122 A B C D E
23 A B C D E	48 A B C D E	73 A B C D E	98 A B C D E	123 A B C D E
24 A B C D E	49 A B C D E	74 A B C D E	99 A B C D E	124 A B C D E
25 A B C D E	50 A B C D E	75 A B C D E	100 A B C D E	125 A B C D E

ANSWER SHEET

T NO. ______________ PART ________ TITLE OF POSITION ______________________________
(AS GIVEN IN EXAMINATION ANNOUNCEMENT - INCLUDE OPTION, IF ANY)

CE OF EXAMINATION ______________________________ (CITY OR TOWN) ______________ (STATE) DATE ______________

RATING

USE THE SPECIAL PENCIL. MAKE GLOSSY BLACK MARKS.

	A	B	C	D	E		A	B	C	D	E		A	B	C	D	E		A	B	C	D	E		A	B	C	D	E
1						26						51						76						101					
2						27						52						77						102					
3						28						53						78						103					
4						29						54						79						104					
5						30						55						80						105					
6						31						56						81						106					
7						32						57						82						107					
8						33						58						83						108					
9						34						59						84						109					
10						35						60						85						110					

Make only ONE mark for each answer. Additional and stray marks may be counted as mistakes. In making corrections, erase errors COMPLETELY.

	A	B	C	D	E		A	B	C	D	E		A	B	C	D	E		A	B	C	D	E		A	B	C	D	E
11						36						61						86						111					
12						37						62						87						112					
13						38						63						88						113					
14						39						64						89						114					
15						40						65						90						115					
16						41						66						91						116					
17						42						67						92						117					
18						43						68						93						118					
19						44						69						94						119					
20						45						70						95						120					
21						46						71						96						121					
22						47						72						97						122					
23						48						73						98						123					
24						49						74						99						124					
25						50						75						100						125					